MARTYR
OF THE
AMAZON

MARTYR
OF THE
AMAZON

The Life of Sister Dorothy Stang

Roseanne Murphy, S.N.D. de N.

ORBIS BOOKS
Maryknoll, New York 10545

Second Printing, December 2007

Published by Orbis Books, Maryknoll, NY 10545-0308.

Manufactured in the United States of America.

Library of Congress Cataloging-in-Publication Data

Murphy, Roseanne, 1932–
  Martyr of the Amazon : the life of Sister Dorothy Stang / Roseanne Murphy.
       p. cm.
  ISBN 978-1-57075-735-8
  1. Stang, Dorothy (Dorothy Mae), d. 2005. 2. Sisters of Notre Dame de Namur—United States—Biography. 3. Sisters of Notre Dame de Namur—Brazil—Biography. I. Title.

BX4705.S7938M87 2007
271'.97—dc22
[B]
                                    2007006877

*This book is dedicated to
two Sisters of Notre Dame de Namur,
Elizabeth Marie Bowyer and Joan Krimm,
whose love for Dorothy impels them to keep her story alive,
and to all the Sisters in Brazil who carry on her work.*

CONTENTS

FOREWORD

It is not every day that we can know a person like Sister Dorothy Mae Stang. A Sister of Notre Dame de Namur, Sister Dorothy was so steeped in the Gospel that every fiber of her being radiated love, concern, and care for God's "little ones."

Sister Dorothy was killed in an attempt to stop her four-decade-long fight for the poor and oppressed of Brazil. Hired assassins shot her as she walked down a dirt road in the Amazon forest on her way to a meeting with peasant farmers who had been constantly harassed by illegal loggers and ranchers.

By telling her story, this book makes it possible for us to know Sister Dorothy. It helps us to understand her Gospel mission, a ministry rooted in the Word of God. We can learn how her ministry radiated her love of God and God's love of the forgotten and voiceless. And we can teach our children why our world needs people like Sister Dorothy Stang.

If for no other reason, this book must be written. It must tell the story of Sister Dorothy Mae Stang, this woman of God, her journey, her faith, and her love, because we owe it to those who come after us. Sister Roseanne Murphy, also a Sister of Notre Dame de Namur, has captured Sister Dorothy's life as she lived it. She explains how Sister Dorothy grew in faith and knowledge of God and came to realize that all of creation was a reflection of God's beauty.

You will see how Dorothy stood in awe of the wonders of God's creation—how she loved the majestic trees of the Amazon forest, the power of the Amazon River, the gentle steams crisscrossing the bed of the forest, the beautiful songs of the birds and the glorious colors of the animals as they romped through the forest; how she gazed into the eyes of the simple people whom she loved and saw in them the reflection of God. One could say that Sister Dorothy was enamored of God's creation.

But, at the same time, we see that Dorothy was sickened by the oppression of the poor. She was angered by the destruction of the rainforest. She had a passion and a dream to work toward the day when all of God's children would have enough to eat, a decent and safe home to live in, and the opportunity for an education and health care. And she dedicated her life to the accomplishment of that dream as she worked for and with the poor in the Amazon forest.

Sister Dorothy knew that her life was in danger. She knew she was on a death list. But knowing this did not stop her. She continued to teach sustainable farming. She continued to found base ecclesial communities wherever she encountered a cluster of families living in the forest. She continued to plead with the government to give deeds to the people to whom they had given land and to protect these families from constant harassment at the hands of the loggers and ranchers.

This is the story of Dorothy's love. It is a story of courage and integrity, of struggle, dedication, and suffering, and, in the end, of martyrdom. It is a story of true Gospel living, a story each of us should experience and strive to imitate in our own surroundings.

Read her story and feel the love, passion, and compassion of one who knew how to live and how to die in the Lord.

Sister Joan Krimm, S.N.D. de N.

ACKNOWLEDGMENTS

When I began to write the story of Sister Dorothy Stang, I never dreamed how far her life would take me into the mind and heart of a woman who knew how to believe and how to love. Her courage and passion for justice shine out from those who knew her and worked with her. The Sisters of Notre Dame de Namur in Brazil, who accepted me and allowed me to write Dorothy's story for them, have given me an honor and trust for which I will be forever grateful. In particular, I am indebted to Sister Jo Anne Depweg in Belém, Sister Jane Dwyer and Sister Katy Webster in Anapu, and Sister Rita Raboin in Brevis. The hospitality of these sisters was magnanimous. They made my visit to Brazil productive by teaching me a great deal about the world in which Dorothy poured out her life. Sister Judith Clemens, my interpreter, made the trip so pleasant by her gracious approach to all those in Brazil who wondered what this American nun was doing, that she inspired them to be completely open, trusting me to tell a story that would be true to their experience of Dorothy. The people who worked with Dorothy in the Amazon were eager to share their experience of her and to let me know of their love for this extraordinary woman.

But this book would never have been completed without the help and encouragement of Sister Elizabeth Marie Bowyer and Sister Joan Krimm, whose love for Dorothy is contagious. Their dedication to keeping her memory alive has led them to spend countless hours sharing Dorothy's story with hundreds of people and groups, explaining that we must not forget why Dorothy was killed and how important her work was for the world. They have inspired many people to become more active in working for justice in Brazil and in facing the reality of global warming that is in large part due to the destruction of the Amazon forest that Dorothy loved so much. They were my mentors during the writing of this book, and I am deeply grateful to them.

Nearly all of the references used in writing Dorothy's story are from primary sources, such as her letters, interviews with those who knew her, and reports sent back to the Sisters of Notre Dame Province Center in Cincinnati, Ohio. Sister Louanna Orth, the archivist for the province, was extremely generous with all the materials I needed for the book. Her archives contain volumes of letters, testimonies, and news reports from all over the world about Dorothy, and everything was made available to me.

I was privileged to have interviewed her brothers, Tom and David Stang, and her sisters, Barbara Stang Richardson, Norma Stang, and Marguerite Stang Hohm. I visited Arizona with Sister Paula Marie Becker who went with Sister Dorothy on her first "mission" assignment to Most Holy Trinity School there. We met with many of Dorothy's former students who shared their stories with us. Sister Paula Marie made the trip possible and profitable as well as fun. Sister Barbara English faithfully wrote the unpublished story of the early days of the Sisters of Notre Dame de Namur in Brazil. The information in her work was invaluable to me. In addition, she generously made time to translate for me the interviews she had with Dorothy in 2003.

It was my very good fortune that a group of graduate students from American University's School of International Service in Washington, DC, decided to write "Dorothy Stang: Struggling for Sustainable Development in the Brazilian Amazon" as part of their thesis for the course entitled "Micropolitics of Development" offered by the International Development Program. Their unpublished manuscript, which was produced under the direction of Dr. Miguel Carter, covered critical areas of the political and economic influences that shaped the climate in which Dorothy worked. I am, indeed, indebted to their work.

I am grateful to Robert Ellsberg, publisher of Orbis Books, who has been supportive and patient while working with me. And last, but certainly no less important, I am deeply grateful to the Julie Community at the Province Center of the Sisters of Notre Dame de Namur in Cincinnati, who took me in as one of their own, encouraged and supported me during the writing of the book, and whose love made it very difficult to leave them when I was finished.

PROLOGUE

She must have had a premonition that something was going to happen that weekend. That's what Ivan thinks. He was the farmer who drove her out to Boa Esperança, a remote settlement in the Amazon forest, where Sister Dorothy Stang was to attend a meeting of poor farmers. He remembers that Dorothy was unusually pensive that day and that she said, "If anything happens, I hope it happens to me. The others have their families."

Ivan knew there was trouble brewing. Tensions between the poor farmers and wealthy ranchers and developers who wanted the farmers' land were reaching a dangerous point. That was the reason for the meeting. As he drove her to Boa Esperança, Ivan assured her that "they wouldn't do anything to a nun." That's what he believed.

But the next morning, February 12, 2005, as she was walking alone through the forest, Dorothy's way was blocked by two gunmen. From the plastic shoulder bag she always carried she produced maps and documents to prove that the disputed area had been designated by the government as a reserve for the landless poor. One of the men asked her if she had a weapon. She smiled and removed her Bible. "This is my only weapon," she said, and then proceeded to read from the Beatitudes: "Blessed are the poor in spirit...Blessed are those who hunger and thirst for justice...Blessed are the peacemakers; they shall be called children of God."

As she turned to leave, one of the men called out to her. The other drew his gun, and when she looked back he shot her through her upraised hand, still clutching her Bible. He

1

continued to fire, six times in all. Afterward, both men ran into the bushes and then fled to the ranch of one of the men who had hired them.

In retrospect, it seemed that all her life had led to this encounter on a lonely path in the Amazon forest she had fought so hard to preserve. Where had that path begun? In her decision to follow the farmers ever deeper into the forest and to stand by them in their struggle for justice? In her response, forty years earlier, to a call for missioners to Brazil? Or in her faithful response to an even earlier call?

1

CALLED TO MISSION

Few people were surprised when Dorothy Mae Stang, at the age of sixteen, sent in her application to the Sisters of Notre Dame de Namur. At least one of those few was her younger sister, Barbara, who wondered why Dorothy would do such a crazy thing. After all, she had a boyfriend, she loved school, and she was involved in so many activities she enjoyed.

At the time Dorothy was only a junior at the sisters' Julienne High School in Dayton, Ohio. But her best friend, Joan Krimm, who was a senior, had already applied to join the congregation and Dorothy was determined to go with her. "You are not going to enter without me," she had told her friend. And though her father thought she might be a bit young for such an important decision, her mother did not seem to mind. In fact, Edna McCloskey Stang was rather pleased that her daughter wanted to become a sister. Both parents were deeply religious and reasoned that if Dorothy felt a call to religious life, she would discover during her first few years with the sisters whether she had a genuine vocation.

From early childhood Dorothy had shown signs of a generous spirit. As one of the middle children in a family of nine siblings, she had had many opportunities to give of herself in helping her mother care for the younger children and her father in working on the farm where they lived outside of town. Lieutenant Colonel Henry Stang was a career military man whose main work in the Air Force had been as a chemical engineer. His German background had helped to fashion him into a well-disciplined man who expected no less from his children. When his own father died, Henry had assumed responsibility for his mother and younger siblings, and he had done the same when his wife's father died. Eventually, with the arrival of his own children, Henry was supporting three families; he felt it was his duty to provide for all of them. Dorothy absorbed his dedication to duty and purpose, even though she also displayed her mother's sense of play and lightheartedness. From her father she learned the rudiments of farming, while absorbing his deep appreciation for the wonders of nature and the natural beauty around them. As an adult, she claimed that she had gotten large hands from pulling weeds in the family's garden.

Both Henry and Edna instilled in their family a strong faith, nourished when possible by daily Mass and evening rosaries. At church on Sundays each child was given an envelope with a dime to be put in the offertory basket. Both parents took leadership positions in St. Rita's Parish; each year Edna was in charge of the kitchen for the annual orphans' home picnic and the church's Fall Festival, organizing twenty or thirty women to feed about two thousand people, while Henry ran the bingo games. The events routinely involved a friendly competition to see which of them could raise the most money. Edna invariably won.

Their home was always open to visitors and to those in need. It was not unusual for the Stang family to take in people struggling to get back on their feet. The children observed the compassion and generosity of their parents, absorbing the lessons for themselves. Henry and Edna made it quite clear that charity was at the heart of their faith and that giving to others was an essential sign of being a Christian.

Although she was an obedient and devoted daughter, Dorothy was not without her moments of minor rebellion. One day, her mother told her to practice the piano. Dorothy had just received a new bike and was anxious to ride it. The piano was in a room on the first floor, near a window. Dorothy parked the bike outside this window. Then she went inside and, after practicing for a few minutes, she stood up, climbed out the window, got on the bike, and started down the driveway. When she turned to see if her mother had observed her escape, her front wheel hit a rock, sending her plummeting over the handlebars. She landed on her face. With her front tooth broken, a contrite and bloodied Dorothy went back inside to finish her practice. For the rest of her life, an unreliable cap on her tooth served to remind her that all our choices have consequences. It was a lesson she frequently shared with her students.

During her high school years, Dorothy was very active in sports and student organizations. She was invited to become part of a select group of students in the Young Christian Student (YCS) movement where they learned to "observe, judge, and act." The emphasis of this group was to deepen their spiritual lives through prayer and the study of scripture and then to become leaders in their social groups and so to draw others to Christ. YCS was fashioned after the "cell movement" used by the young Communists in recruiting new members. Msgr. Joseph Cardijn, founder of the movement in Belgium in the 1920s, believed that if Communist youth were successful in influencing their peers, young Christian workers ought to be able to do the same. The movement was adapted for high school and college students in the 1940s in the United States.

Dorothy became a natural leader in YCS, which stimulated her desire to spread the good news of the Gospel to others. This desire was further fired by a song sung by most of the students in Catholic high schools of the day: "An army of youth flying the standards of truth, we're fighting for Christ the Lord." Rallies of Catholic students often drew thousands of young people together, and they would sing this song with great enthusiasm. "On earth's battlefield, never a vantage we'll yield, as dauntlessly on we sing, comrades true, dare and do, 'neath the Queen's white and blue, for our flag, for our faith, for Christ the King." It was a rousing song, and Dorothy internalized the message.

All through her years at Julienne, the Notre Dame sisters had stressed the importance of praying for the missions and supporting them. It was a natural outcome of the vision of St. Julie Billiart who had founded the sisters at the beginning of the nineteenth century. Facing the ravages of war brought about by the French Revolution and Napoleon, St. Julie saw the need of the poor for education. She encouraged the members of her congregation to teach the poor the value of their souls and their dignity before God. Julie often said, "Give me the poor, only the poor," and began schools in France and Belgium for poor girls only. Julie knew that there were tens of thousands of orphans in her country. Her heart melted at the sight of so many children, especially young girls, abandoned and neglected. "It seems to me," she wrote to a good friend, "that I should like to go throughout the whole universe to tear these poor little creatures out of the clutches of the demon, to teach them the value of their souls." She was convinced that the members of her congregation were to go wherever they were needed in the world to teach the poor about their dignity and God's love for them. It is not surprising, then, that the Sisters of Notre Dame stressed the importance of praying for the missions and helping to support them.

At Dorothy's school there were mission fairs and mission days. During Lent, Dorothy and her classmates were encouraged to make sacrifices by depriving themselves of something they would like and giving the money they saved for the "pagan babies." The money went to the Propagation of the Faith, a church organization that provided support to missionaries all over the world. The Maryknoll Fathers provided the school with movies depicting the work of their missionaries in China, Africa, and Latin America. Seeing children in such dire circumstances touched Dorothy's heart, inspiring her to "do something" for them. Competition among classes to see how much money they could raise for the missions only increased Dorothy's desire to be more generous in helping the poor in foreign countries. In addition, the diocese had mission appeals and parishes displayed posters showing scenes from mission countries. Sometimes Dorothy even conned some small change out of her younger brothers and sisters, persuading them that they could walk to choir practice instead of riding the bus.

Religion classes also stressed service and generosity. Pope Pius XII had written a new encyclical on the Mystical Body of Christ. The doctrine emphasized the "power of one person" to influence the whole of humanity by bringing into the world either love or its opposite. In the midst of the horrors of World War II, the pope's words encouraged the faithful to realize that even though there were tremendous problems of violence, greed, and hatred in the world, one person really could make a difference.

Dorothy attended carefully to all these messages. At the top of her application to join the Sisters of Notre Dame, she wrote, "I want to be a missionary in China." She did not know at the time that the sisters had been forced to withdraw from China during the Second World War. However, her application was accepted and on July 26, 1948, less than two months after her seventeenth birthday, Dorothy Mae Stang, her best friend, Joan Krimm, along with fourteen other young women, presented themselves at the novitiate of the Sisters of Notre Dame de Namur in Reading, Ohio.

The spirituality of the community—typical of religious congregations of that era—emphasized the development of a strong relationship with God and a rejection of the "standards of the world." The new members were to concentrate on growing in their prayer life and practicing acts of mortification, which would restrain any desire for worldly pleasures.

Dorothy and Joan were ready for this. Having read the lives of the saints who had practiced heroic acts of penance, they were ready for "anything," or at least they thought they were. When they were shown their places in the dormitory the day they arrived, they were shocked and disappointed to discover that beds were provided, even if they were only furnished with straw mattresses. They had expected—and half-hoped, in their initial flush of enthusiasm—that they would be sleeping on the floor. Soon enough, however, when they were told that they were to keep silence throughout the day, only speaking during two periods of recreation, they realized that their asceticism was of a different but just as difficult a sort. Sister Ann Louise, their directress, insisted that the new members learn quickly that they were to work hard at their studies to prepare themselves for their future tasks. In fact, she did not approve of any new member who was not working or studying all the time. It turned out, indeed, that the asceticism of the postulancy—even if undramatic—was as rigorous as anything those "heroic saints" had endured.

The days went by quickly for the postulants, as their schedules were full and they were always engaged in work, study, or prayers. Meanwhile, Dorothy, who had completed only three years of high school, still had to finish her final year. In addition to studying everything her fellow postulants were assigned, she had to take a number of additional courses before she could receive her diploma from Julienne High School. She did this by attending summer school before she entered and completing the rest of her requirements during her six months as a postulant.

The postulants were united by a strong sense of loyalty to one another. One of them had come from a family that had bitterly opposed her becoming a sister and had threatened to disown her. She did not receive any mail from her family and was essentially cut off from them. Her fellow postulants decided that they would not open their own mail until she got a letter, too. It was months before Sister Ann Louise discovered that most of the group had had no news from home. Finally, in December, the directress told the group that they should read their mail. It was then that the postulant discovered what her friends had sacrificed for her.

While the postulants were expected to spend most of their time working on their assignments, Dorothy and Joan managed on more than one occasion to slip through the gym into the apple orchard. Dorothy would climb a tree and throw apples down to Joan. Then the two of them would sit under the tree and eat of the forbidden fruit. When the postulants were told that if they wished to receive the habit they would have to ask their directress for the privilege, Dorothy and Joan decided they would go together. They knelt before Sister Ann Louise and asked to be given the habit. They prefaced their request by admitting their "crime" of apple stealing and proceeded to tell her they did not think she would be able to give them permission to continue in the order. To their surprise, they were permitted to receive the habit of the Sisters of Notre Dame. Each of them, as was the custom, took a new name to symbolize her new life as a religious woman. Dorothy was given the name "Sister Mary Joachim" and Joan became "Sister Mary Carl."

Now, as novices, they would learn more about the history of the congregation and receive intensive spiritual instruction. This was during the pre–Vatican II period, when the emphasis on spiritual growth tended to be introspective and ascetic, defined as concentrating on one's pursuit of perfection and overcoming attachments to one's will. The three characteristics of the sisters of Notre Dame were simplicity, obedience, and charity. Simplicity was defined as openness and sincerity; there were to be no false pretenses or artificial airs. The sisters were to be obedient to their superiors, trusting that God would reveal His will for them through those who had been appointed to places of authority. And their charity was to be boundless, since they were to see Christ in those they served and in each other. It was a lofty goal, and they were to strive to "be perfect."

In fact, much time and effort went into the pursuit of perfection. Nurtured on spiritual books outlining progress in the spiritual life and the lives of the saints, novices in all congregations often worked so hard at becoming "perfect" that they could even have become competitive in their search for that elusive goal. Dorothy already possessed a strong sense of duty; she worked hard at fulfilling the expectations of her novice directress and was rewarded by becoming a somewhat favored protégée. However, there was one occasion when she and Joan simply drew the line.

It was an annual custom to honor the superior on her feast day with original poems or skits and conclude with the reading of a letter of gratitude. In addition, each sister would approach the superior and, as a sign of appreciation, kiss her lightly on both cheeks, European style. Dorothy and Joan decided they simply "couldn't do that." Before the ceremony, they found the key to a supply closet and, at the moment during the feast when all the sisters stood for the sign of appreciation, they slipped out the back of the room, entered the closet, and locked the door. Listening carefully so they would emerge from the closet in time to fall in line with their companions on their way to the special feast-day meal, they heard the sisters disappearing down the corridor. It was completely silent for a few moments, and just as they decided they could leave the closet, they heard footsteps coming toward them. They looked at each other in dismay and suddenly heard Sister Ann Louise's voice say, "Unlock that door and come out of the closet." Terrified, they emerged, expecting a severe rebuke, but only heard, "Now go to lunch." To their delight and surprise, that was the end of the episode.

The first year of the novitiate, called the "canonical year," was devoted to the study of theology, spirituality, and the religious life. The second year continued some of these courses but, in addition, the novices would be given college courses and instruction in methods of teaching. They would be sent out into the schools to observe experienced teachers working with their students. There was greater emphasis on the significance of the vowed life and what it meant to give oneself completely to God through the congregation. Gradually, the day on which the novices would make their first vows grew closer. The excitement of making their vows, exchanging the white veil of the novice for the black veil of the "professed" sisters, could be felt among the "second year" novices.

For a while, Dorothy went through a period of serious reflection on what she was about to do. During the retreat to prepare the novices for vows, she withdrew from her group for a short period and was allowed more time to think about making this religious commitment. It was a serious choice, one that could not be lightly made. Somehow, Dorothy needed the extra time for prayer and discernment, but eventually she emerged more certain than ever that this was to be her life and that she would live rooted in faith that God would see her through the days ahead. She had learned that her two twin brothers, David and Tom, were both going to enter the seminary. In the fall of 1951, Tom Stang entered the Precious Blood Seminary and David Stang entered the Maryknoll Seminary. Her sister, Norma, had entered the Precious Blood Sisters. While her younger siblings were about to begin their own spiritual journeys in religious life, Dorothy was preparing to make her first vows.

Dorothy and the other members of her group made their vows during Mass in January 1951. With lighted candles in their hands, they knelt at the altar rail as each one pronounced her vows of poverty, chastity, and obedience to God, to the representative of the church, and to the Sisters of Notre Dame. The ceremony was beautiful. These young women had heard the words of Christ in John's Gospel, "You have not chosen me, but I have chosen you to go out and bear fruit, fruit that will last" (John 15:16).

The taking of vows marked a profound transition from the cloister of novitiate days. Each newly professed sister was given her first "mission." Dorothy, Sister Mary Joachim, was sent to teach third grade at St. Victor's School in Calumet City, Illinois. Joan, Sister Mary Carl, was sent to Columbus,

Ohio, to St. Patrick's Elementary School, to teach fifty-five children from kindergarten to the second grade, all in one classroom. The two friends parted wondering if they would ever live in the same convent again.

When Sister Mary Joachim reached St. Victor's School on January 23, 1951, she found that she was replacing a sister who had fallen ill and that the community was planning to move into a new convent. In the annals of the community it was written, "It's an ill wind that blows no good. Sister Superior Provincial has sent us a young professed, Sister Mary Joachim, to help." She found herself in a typical Chicago third-grade classroom, teaching about seventy students while helping the sisters prepare to move to the new convent. Fortunately, there were experienced teachers in the community who could mentor the young sister and help her adjust to the classroom. Because of her generous nature and her good sense of humor, she was able to adapt to the changes and the challenges of her new assignment. She proved to be a "natural teacher" and her love for the children was obvious from the beginning.

By August, only eight months later, Sister Mary Joachim was transferred to St. Alexander School in Villa Park, Illinois, to teach fourth grade for a year and then fifth grade the following year. In 1953, when a call for volunteers came from the provincial superior for sisters who would be willing to go on "mission" to a new school in Arizona, Sister Mary Joachim was one of the first to apply. It was a great distance from Ohio. It was also a great distance from the mission in China, where Dorothy had originally dreamed of serving. But, no matter, it was still an opportunity to go on "mission."

2
ARIZONA INTERLUDE

From the early 1940s there had been a mission church located in Sunnyslope, Arizona, a sparsely populated area outside of Phoenix. Fr. Alfred Monaghan, S.J., came regularly from the parish church of St. Xavier's in town to minister to the sick and those confined to their homes. Operating at first out of a rented storefront, the congregation in Sunnyslope finally built a small, concrete block chapel on three acres of land, purchased with the assistance of a $1,000 grant from the Extension Society, a group dedicated to sponsoring "home missions." The priest simply transferred the name printed on the storefront, "Our Lady of the Wayside," to the new chapel.

By 1951, the size of the congregation had grown so that Bishop Daniel J. Gercke of Tucson established it as a parish and named it Most Holy Trinity Parish, with Fr. Neil McHugh as pastor. The new pastor inherited an enormous debt of $14,000, which was soon to grow even larger. There was no permanent church. There was no school, nor were there nuns to staff it. There was no convent, or even a rectory. The priest lived in a rented house. Eventually plans were made to to buy nine and a half acres of a neighboring grapefruit grove for the parish. The sale was contingent on the owners being able to harvest their last crop before the buyers took over the land.

In February of 1953, Bishop Gercke received word from Sister Berchmans of Mary, the provincial superior of the Ohio Province of the Sisters of Notre Dame de Namur, that she could send four or five sisters to teach in the school at Sunnyslope. The pastor hesitated at first, wondering if the 350 parish families would be able to support the additional financial burden and if they could build a school and convent in six months. But the consensus of the parishioners was to go ahead, and the construction of a four-classroom building with an outside covered corridor began. It was, indeed, missionary territory.

In August of that year, four sisters left Mount Notre Dame in Reading, Ohio, for the Cincinnati Union Terminal. Sister Barbara Louise, who had been assigned to join the community in Glendale, Sister Paula Marie, Sister Ann Timothy, and Sister Mary Joachim (Dorothy) were surrounded by family members, Sister Berchmans of Mary, and a few nuns who had come to see the four sisters off. It was the first train ride for most of them. The Santa Fe line traversed the southern route through hundreds of miles of magnificent scenery. As the sisters retired for the first night, they heard Dorothy call to them, "You've got to see this full moon over the Mississippi River. Come down to my berth and just see its beauty." They all piled onto the small bed and gazed at the great river reflecting the glory of the full moon.

When the sisters arrived in Phoenix, the superior of the convent in Glendale, Sister Marie Tarpy, and their new superior, Sister Angelina Wald, were waiting for them. They all set off for Our Lady of Perpetual Help convent, which, with its school, had been opened by the Sisters of Notre Dame in 1950. The members of the new community were told that, because their convent in Sunnyslope was not yet ready for them, they would be staying in the guest rooms of the Sisters of the Good Shepherd, whose work was with young women who had been in trouble with the law or who had been sent to them by the courts. The sisters had a good laugh at the thought that they would be starting out in a place for "wayward women."

Each day, the sisters went to Most Holy Trinity to help get the school ready. Sister Mary Joachim immediately got to work sanding the old desks, which had been procured when the public schools were getting rid of them, while Sister Ann Timothy and Sister Paula Marie varnished the tops. The sisters quickly established good rapport with people in the parish, who volunteered their talent and hundreds of hours of their time to get the school and the convent ready to open. The parishioners were so happy to have the sisters that they began collecting canned goods for the convent as well as bringing needed supplies for the school.

Within a month of their arrival, the sisters moved into the small convent that was actually two prefabricated houses joined together. Each house had three bedrooms, one of which was turned into a small chapel where the sisters had morning and evening prayers together. Gradually, the community "settled in" to the routine of running a new school, which opened on September 14.

The first year there were 129 students in grades one through six in four classrooms. Sister Angelina taught fifth and sixth grades and was principal and superior. Sister Paula Marie had third and fourth grades, Sister Mary Joachim had second grade, and Sister Ann Timothy had first grade. Each year, the sisters stayed with their original classes, and the number of students continued to grow. Within four years Sister Paula Marie had seventy students and Sister Mary Joachim had as many. She taught grades two, three, four, and five consecutively with the same students.

The first day of school started with some of the children having a grapefruit fight in the schoolyard. They were hurling grapefruits at each other when Sister Angelina came outside and, in a loud voice yelled, "You children get into this school *right now!*"

The fight stopped instantly. In no time at all, the children were seated quietly at their desks. It was very clear that Sister Angelina was in charge. Later in the school year, the sisters had the children harvest the grapefruits and sell them by the bag at Mass on Sunday. The proceeds were used to buy supplies for migrant workers.

At the end of the second year, the provincial, Sister Berchmans of Mary, paid a visit to Sunnyslope. Arriving on a blistering hot day, she realized that the black habits the sisters were wearing were unbearable in the desert heat. So, she had a sister from Cincinnati sent to Sunnyslope to make light grey habits with white veils for all the Sisters of Notre Dame in Arizona. The new habits proved to be much more comfortable in the relentless sun. The black habits had collected dust so fast that they had had to be frequently washed and had begun to take on a rust color. But even all the washing didn't get rid of the dust. Someone had suggested dousing the habits in gasoline. This had worked, but it had also left the sisters smelling like a filling station. The grey habits were a welcome relief.

When her former students reminisced about "Sister Mary Jo" (as they quickly came to call her), they immediately recalled her kindness and her love for them. She was only twenty-two when she started teaching at Most Holy Trinity. The boys could not get over how well she could throw a football. She would hitch her long skirt up a bit so she could run faster. One day, after she had caught the ball and was running down the field, her veil and bonnet went flying off. The boys were shocked and embarrassed, but Sister Mary Jo simply snatched the headpiece, put it back on her head, and went on playing. They thought that was great. Essentially serving as the school coach, she also taught the girls softball and played with them as well. The students' lasting visual memory was of Sister Mary Jo, with veil flying, running across a field or around the bases.

Most of the children were from middle- and lower-middle-class families, although there were one or two whose fathers were professionals. The tuition was very low and the school increased in size each year as the parish added classrooms and more teachers came.

Luis Aguilar was a second grader when he started at the school. One of only a very few number of Mexican children there, he was short and spoke very broken English. One day, Sister Mary Jo came up to his desk before recess and, in her very limited Spanish, said to him, "You don't understand everything, do you?"

Luis shook his head. "No, I don't."

Gently she said, "I want to help you with your English, so you stay with me when the others go out for recess." She kept him and two other students at recess time to coach them until they could speak English well. When she realized that some of the other students did not play with Luis because they could not understand him, she announced one day to the class, "Luis can speak *two* languages. He is bilingual. Isn't that wonderful?" Luis felt "nine feet tall" as the other children looked on with admiration. From that time on he was "in." He never forgot her kindness.

Nancy, another former student, recalls that the desks were old, with folding seats that were left up when no one was in the room. One day, she came running in from recess and, not realizing that the seat was still up, sat down quickly and hit her head hard on the back of the desk. Though it hurt her terribly and she sobbed with the pain, some of the other children snickered and pointed at her. Sister Mary Jo quickly came down the aisle, held Nancy close, and rubbed the back of her head to comfort her. She also calmly explained to the other children that it was all right to cry when you are hurt and very unkind to laugh at people who are injured and in pain. Her loving concern for the hurt child left an indelible impression on the whole class.

Another time some of the girls had gathered at recess and were surreptitiously devouring a copy of the forbidden *Mad* magazine when Sister Mary Jo approached them. They had been looking at a cartoon of an overweight and slovenly woman standing in her slip by a sink full of dishes as dirty children cried at her feet. It was an image of a woman whose life was out of control. The girls were giggling at this, and when Sister Mary Jo asked them what they were doing, they cringed. They expected the worst, thinking they would be assigned a five-hundred-word essay on why they shouldn't be reading *Mad*, or told to weed the garden, or to bang chalk out of the erasers. But instead, as one of the students recalled, "what Sister did was to take us aside in an affectionate and confidential way, as if to share a secret, and said that we should respect ourselves as women, and not allow such negative images of women in our minds or in the minds of others. Her message struck home mostly because of her totally caring way of delivering it." It was a teaching moment that forged a greater bond between the teacher and her students.

Sister Mary Jo started a club for altar boys and called it "The Knights of the Altar." It was a serious club that made significant demands of a boy if he wanted to serve Mass. She told the boys what was expected, and if they wished to belong to this prestigious group, they had to pass an examination.

The levels of "knighthood" started with Page, then Squire, then Knight, and, if you were really good, "Grand Knight." In order to join, you had to have acquired at least two hundred points by demonstrating that you could say the responses to the prayers of the Mass in Latin, knew the names of the various vestments the priest wore, and could identify the vessels used on the altar. If you were dependable and served all your assigned Masses, you could take the next examination. Success on this examination, as well as completion of other requirements, would enable you to earn more points. After acquiring three hundred points you could be a Squire, four hundred points a Knight, and five hundred points a Grand Knight.

Eventually a boy would know all the prayers of the Mass in English and Latin, the names of the parts of the church (the nave, the transept, etc.), the names of the twelve apostles, the books of the New Testament, the priest's vestments and the order in which he put them on and took them off, and the prayers he said when getting robed for Mass. All the information was typed on twelve legal-sized pages run off on the purple-print mimeograph machine. The student just kept building up his knowledge as he went through the packet of material. Before he could advance, however, he had to prove that he was dependable and punctual. Jim Mitchell remembers:

> As far as the processions as such, we practiced for hours, or so it seemed... I remember we would file in in ascending order of height (my cousin and I were the shortest right through eighth grade, so we got to be acolytes and carry the candles and lead the processions). The hardest part was that we were right behind the Knights of Columbus, who were nice, but they wore those capes and plumes, and they would swish them around so it was a challenge to keep your candle lit. We would file in in that order and march, counting to three before moving forward so we would be evenly spaced. You also somehow kept an eye on your partner who would be directly across from you going up the aisle. Then Sr. Mary Joachim would click the clicker, we would genuflect, count three seconds —one thousand one, one thousand two... Then she would click again and we would rise, the rows would part, and we would process across the front of the first pew and then enter the pew from the opposite side. Whenever we would have to stand, genuflect, or walk, she would click the clicker and we would follow the three-second rule.

The boys vied with each other to see how perfect they could be and there was competition among them to get the "best" Masses, such as school Masses and Masses for special holidays. After Holy Thursday Mass, when there was Adoration of the Blessed Sacrament all night, a number of the boys tried to get the 2:00–3:00 AM slot so they could brag the next day about being at church in the middle of the night, much to the chagrin of the fathers who had to get up and drive them there. Shoes were to be polished, hands were to be clean, and the Knights were to be models of behavior. Sister Mary Jo made it sound so wonderful that the boys were anxious to be Knights in her club. Progression in "knighthood" was accompanied by the conferral of a small medal attached to a "K of A" pin decorated by two knights on either side of a chalice, the badge of honor of the Knights of the Altar.

During the summers in the first few years, Sister Mary Joachim, Sister Paula Marie, and other sisters would go to Albuquerque, New Mexico, to attend the College of St. Joseph on the Rio Grande for six weeks to complete their college studies. They took courses in Spanish, Latin American history, the sciences, educational methods, and a variety of other subjects. During her last two summer sessions, Sister Mary Joachim attended the College of Notre Dame in Belmont, California, conducted by the Sisters of Notre Dame, where she received a bachelor of arts degree in English and history with the class of 1964.*

The sisters were always busy. In addition to preparing their classes, keeping their religious schedule of prayer, attending Mass each day in Our Lady of the Wayside chapel, and teaching in the school, they also taught religion classes for the children in public schools (on Saturday mornings for children from the first to the eighth grades and one night a week for the teenagers). In addition to that, Fr. McHugh and Fr. Gillespie, the associate pastor, asked them to minister to the migrant workers at a nearby ranch on Friday afternoons.

After school, Fr. Gillespie and the three youngest sisters would pile into the parish station wagon and drive out to the ranch to teach migrant children about their faith. The sisters wanted the Mexican workers who did not come to church regularly to know that they were a part of the parish and that the church cared for them. It was the first time the nuns had seen such poverty. The people lived in shacks with dirt floors.

---

*The College of Notre Dame is now called Notre Dame de Namur University.

They had no electricity, no running water, and no indoor toilets. Near the homes there was an irrigation ditch where the workers could get water. Often the only food available to them was some leftover vegetables. The farm produced lettuce and onions, and one time the sisters observed that a family had only a head of lettuce for their dinner.

Dorothy came to love her work with the migrant laborers. She and the other sisters worked closely with the members of the parish in providing aid for them. She started taking some of the eighth-grade girls with her to help teach catechism to the children who came out of their huts and sat on the ground to listen to the sisters. Her students also helped in distributing clothes and food to the people in need. It was clear to her that teaching religion had to involve action as well as words. Her bedroom was usually filled with boxes of clothing to take to the poor. Outside the convent, there were stacks of chairs, tables, and other furnishings the parishioners had brought to give to the migrant workers and their families. Sister Mary Jo would try to bring as many of the migrant families into the parish as she could. But most of the time the workers stayed in the fields to work.

There was, however, always a good group for First Holy Communion. Somehow, most of the families managed to get a white dress and veil for their daughters and a suit for their sons. If any family was not able to provide special clothes, the parishioners made sure that the family received them. The mothers would come into the church while the men stayed outside during the Mass, as was the custom in Mexico. It was an especially meaningful and important day for the families and the sisters made it as festive as they could.

After Mass, Sister Mary Jo would invite the families to a little reception and then let them go through the clothing and furnishings to take what they wanted. She was impressed when she saw that they took only what they needed and shared with each other as well. Over the years, since the families stayed only as long as it took to pick a crop, Sister Mary

Jo saw hundreds of families and heard thousands of stories of hardship and heartbreak. It was a struggle for her to learn Spanish, but somehow the workers came to understand her. She grew to love her work in Arizona so much that she was said to have told her sisters, "Someday I want to be buried under a saguaro cactus here."

These were defining days for Sister Mary Joachim. She could not get what she saw and heard out of her mind. She tried to convince the migrant parents that it was essential that the children have an education. The owner of the ranch did see to it that the school bus would come to pick up the children. But because the workers were paid by the number of "pieces" they picked, the children would often be held back from school to help pick vegetables and earn more money for the family. Several times while the sisters were teaching outdoors, they saw crop-dusting planes approaching. Sister Mary Jo would yell at the workers to get down, to come back to the shacks and get the children inside. But the workers would refuse to move, saying that the owner would be angry with them if they left the field. One day after a spraying she became so distraught and frustrated that she broke down and cried.

She saw young babies in cardboard boxes being pulled along behind their mothers as they picked. Often, she had to drive a baby to the hospital because of dehydration from being out in the hot sun too long. One of her students wrote:

> There was a campfire burning and coffee was brewing in a pot. Women prepared beans and tortillas for everyone. Behind the fields of lettuce the sun was beginning to sink, its rays shining pinkly through a heavy cloud of spray as it settled to earth. Suddenly, a woman ran screaming out of one of the shacks with a baby in her arms. The baby's face and arms were blue, and he was limp. Sister began to blow into his mouth as she ran to her car. One of the workers got

in and drove them to the nearest hospital. We all waited quietly for several hours until they returned— without the baby. The mother was frighteningly quiet, as were the younger children who were usually playful and noisy. We sat around the fire until late, until the sky was dark. I couldn't understand most of the Spanish, but I understood that the topic was not catechism. On our way home that night, Sister talked about the power of the workers, and about how standing together for what you believe in and deserve is a very powerful weapon. She explained how racism and capitalism were connected, and how unions could impact change. I will always remember the expression on her face, her dark eyebrows knitted together, her voice low, and how very important this all seemed to her, even though I didn't fully understand.

The stirrings of desire to go to the foreign missions had started burning in Sister Mary Joachim's heart. This was reinforced over some of the summers that she spent in Mexico, teaching poor children catechism and ministering to their needs. One summer, her brother Tom, who had been ordained in 1964, accompanied the sisters to Sonorita, not far over the Mexican border, for the two weeks they were to spend working in the parish there. Once they arrived in the parish, the local priest disappeared. It was annoying to the sisters that the pastor would come back in his air-conditioned car to conduct a funeral, take his stipend, and leave again. Fr. Tom, who could speak Spanish, was essentially the pastor for the whole time they were there. Sister Mary Joachim saw how much needed to be done.

During the 1960s, many Americans were becoming aware of the injustices toward farm workers thanks to Cesar Chavez and his efforts to organize the United Farm Workers Union. Sister Mary Joachim could easily identify with Chavez, who fought to protect the farm workers from being sprayed with pesticides, to give them decent housing and a living wage. A successful national grape boycott, which lasted five years, helped force many growers to negotiate with the union. In the same years, the civil rights movement was highlighting the problem of racism and injustice toward people of color, and awakening the consciences of vast numbers of people. It was becoming clear that people organizing for justice could bring about necessary social change. Meanwhile, in the church, the Second Vatican Council (1962–1965) was inviting all the people of God to work for justice and bring Gospel values into the world. It was a time of enormous energy, idealism, and growth for Americans of all religious traditions.

In 1963, when Pope John XXIII sent out an appeal to all North American religious communities asking them to commit 10 percent of their personnel to serve in Latin America, the major superior of the Sisters of Notre Dame wrote a letter to all the members, asking for volunteers. Sister Mary Joachim, who was at the time superior and principal at Most Holy Trinity, sent in her name immediately. Still, she was surprised when she received a letter in 1966 telling her that she had been chosen to join the second group to go to Brazil. Many of her former students recall how thrilled she was at receiving the news that she was finally going to be able to go to the foreign missions. Even better, she learned that her good friend, Sister Joan Krimm, would be going as well. Her lifelong dream was coming true.

3

BRAZIL BEGINNINGS

Five Sisters of Notre Dame—Sisters Barbara English from Maryland, Marie Heinz from California, Patricia McQuade from Massachusetts, and Joan Krimm and Dorothy from Ohio—arrived in Petrópolis, Brazil, in August 1966. They were to study at the Center for Intercultural Formation (CENFI) located in the mountains above Rio de Janeiro from August to December, 1966. They could stay at the center during the week, but on weekends they had to go into Rio to immerse themselves in the culture and to practice their Portuguese. There were at least sixty new missionaries at the center from various parts of the world and several different religious communities. The Sisters of Notre Dame were the only ones in the traditional habit.

The regimen was intense: for six hours each day they studied Portuguese, the history of Brazil, politics, the various religions and cults of the people, and local customs. They learned that Brazil had been colonized by the "cross and the sword." The Portuguese had brought slaves over from Africa and summarily baptized each one on the ship coming over since, by law, everyone living in Brazil at that time had to be a Catholic. Their baptism, however, was not accompanied by any deeper faith formation. Consequently, the religious faith that developed combined Christians symbols with various native beliefs. Syncretism continued to play a role for large numbers of Brazilian Catholics. Many who attended Catholic

Masses also attended Candomble, Umbanda, or Macumba ceremonies or practiced some form of spiritism.

Two of the new missionaries were French "worker priests." They belonged to a movement that had started in France during the Second World War when some of the clergy took off their clerical collars, got jobs in factories, and attempted to bridge the gap between the church and the world of the workers. These two worker priests began to poke fun at the Sisters of Notre Dame for wearing the habit and challenged the nuns to go mountain climbing with them. Dorothy rose to the challenge and talked her friend Joan into going too. Tucking their long skirts up at the waist, the two nuns kept up with the priests as they went up the mountain and Dorothy was the first one down. She was elated to have "shown them."

It became clear, however, that the habit and the terrain of Brazil did not go together. When it poured rain, the streets became slippery and treacherous. Mud coated the long skirts and the habits simply would not dry.

One day, Dorothy, who was assigned to be the superior of the group, decided that it was time to look for some regular clothes. The sisters went to the marketplace to purchase skirts. They did not even know what sizes to ask for, but simply held the skirts up against them to see whether they would fit. They also got some white material and found a woman who could make blouses for them. After returning to CENFI, they tried on the skirts and puzzled over which ones they could wear. When the white blouses were finished, they put their outfits together. Various combinations of skirts, white blouses, black long stockings, and black oxford shoes brought howls of laughter and a consensus that they looked horrible. Finally, they decided that they would give their black habits to the seamstress and ask her to make skirts and short veils from them. Then they settled into their new look.

When they sent their pictures to the major superior, Sister Loretta Julia, she gave them permission to continue to wear their new outfits. A few years earlier, Pope Pius XII had asked religious communities to modernize their habits, and by 1966 many religious communities had changed into more modern dress. The Brazil group was among the first in the congregation to follow that recommendation.

Two of the instructors at the center were to become quite prominent in Latin America as early proponents of liberation theology. Fr. Gustavo Gutiérrez and Fr. Jon Sobrino offered courses that addressed the question of how the Gospel should be lived out in countries dominated by a few extremely wealthy families while the majority lived in appalling poverty. It was obvious that the imbalance was due to profound social injustices and was contrary to the teachings of the Gospel. Spurred on by the new vision of the church promulgated by the Second Vatican Council, these instructors taught that Christianity demanded everyone's participation in the struggle for a more just world. As Gustavo Gutiérrez wrote:

> In Latin America, the challenge does not come first and foremost from non-believers but from "non-persons" —that is, those whom the prevailing social order does not acknowledge as persons; the poor, the ex-ploited, those systematically and lawfully stripped of their human status, those who hardly know what a human being is. Non-persons represent a challenge, not primarily to our religious world, but to our eco-nomic, social, political and cultural world. Their ex-istence is a call to revolutionary transformation of the very foundation of our dehumanizing society.

The sisters were beginning to realize the depth of the roots of poverty in Brazil and the enormity of the challenges that awaited them. But, for the moment, they concentrated on try-ing to learn the language, which proved to be very difficult for Dorothy. Sister Barbara English reminisces about those days:

We went to CENFI, the language and acculturation school, and bumbled and fumbled our way through the maze of a new tongue and new culture. Our group led the parties at the school and Dot loved a party. What we learned at CENFI was invaluable. We studied the Vatican documents and steeped ourselves in Brazilian history and the pastoral plan for the church of Brazil. More importantly, we went away with a commitment to respect the Brazilian culture, to question the world around us and understand it through the eyes of the poor.

When the five sisters left CENFI on December 18, their first stop was Recife, where they stayed with the Immaculate Heart of Mary Sisters and met an American priest, Fr. Mahon, who was gathering small groups of people into what he called "Families of God." Each of these groups shared scripture together and discussed how they could apply its teachings to everyday life. It was an early example of the "base ecclesial communities" that would play an enormous role in the renewal of Catholicism throughout Latin America.

From Recife, on December 23, the sisters went to Rosario, a northeastern city in the state of Maranhão, where Marie Heinz would join the local Notre Dame community. After celebrating Christmas together, the four remaining sisters met a driver from Coroatá and began the ten-hour, two hundred mile trip to their new assignment.

When they arrived—their trip delayed by only two flat tires—they were greeted by the two Italian co-pastors from the parish of Our Lady of the Pieta, Fr. Lourenzo and Fr. Gabriel. The priests had prepared for the sisters a house located about a block from the church. Half of the house was somewhat ready for them; the other half was falling down. In a letter to the provincial written on Easter Sunday, 1967, Dorothy wrote about their first days in Coroatá. Describing the house, she wrote:

The other half of our house that never was repaired was causing trouble. The walls were caving in and there were no doors or windows left, as they had been used to repair our side. The bats began to nest, and as we have no ceilings and the walls go up only so high, the bats began to fly across the walls to this side. Also, other rodents, etc., began a little at a time to make themselves present.

The first few days were spent scrubbing and painting the house. Sister Loretta Julia, the general superior of the congregation, had written ahead to the priests to inquire if each sister would have a bed and a dresser. They did. They also had a set of plastic dishes that were especially attractive to the ants. However, they had no pots or pans or kitchen utensils, all of which they had to buy. Later, when the sisters received enough money, they had the "other side" of the house repaired. This provided two large rooms that they used as club rooms for the teenagers who had nowhere else to go. Soon the house became livable and they were ready for the bishop to visit them.

After welcoming the new community, Bishop Motta said, "Thank God you don't have veils!" The truth is that they had saved their new veils from getting covered with dust on the trip and did not have them on when he arrived. They learned later that the bishop's remark came from his experience at a Mass during which a group of women who did not have hats or mantillas used a tablecloth instead. During the celebration, several women sat together under the tablecloth, which they held over their heads like a sheet. At Communion time, the women on the two ends complained loudly that, because they could not adequately cover their heads, they could not receive Communion. After the liturgical renewal of the Second Vatican Council, women were no longer required to cover their heads in church. The bishop wanted the sisters to "prove" that there had been such a change, and thus prevent a recurrence of the tablecloth fiasco. And that is how the sisters came to put aside their veils.

Sister Joan describes what the sisters saw when they went to Mass:

> The church here is like the old woman who lived in the shoe. She has so many children she cannot cope with them. It is not faith that is lacking here—these people have it—but the Church is lacking in her ministry, her guidance, and more important, her love. Yesterday there were crowds at the services, and the edifice is large. The poorest of the poor were there, the most ignorant of the ignorant, the sick and the hungry, but all seeking God to the best of their ability. They pushed, talked, crowded like sardines into a church where they hear their own language but in words they don't understand because it is not the everyday language of the people. At Communion time they shoved and struggled to reach the altar just as though they were trying to reach a bargain basement counter. These children of God who have to fight for their very existence seem to feel they must do the same to receive Him in Holy Communion—one wonders if they really understand what Holy Communion is.

At Mass, the bishop called the sisters into the sanctuary and asked them to say a few words. Since Dorothy was the appointed representative of the group, she was chosen to address the assembly in her new language—an assignment she found very difficult. In her limited Portuguese, she kept saying over and over, "Thank you. We're happy to be here. Thank you very much," which was all she was able to say. Finally, the bishop took over and rescued her by thanking the sisters for coming. Years later, in retelling that story, the community was still laughing about Dorothy's "inaugural address."

Initially the sisters thought that they were going to teach in the school, but the co-pastors asked them instead to concentrate on pastoral work and help develop base ecclesial communities. They wished to evangelize the people who had very little education regarding their religion and to develop leadership among them. There were twelve thousand people in the town and a total of ninety-six thousand in the wider area served by the two priests and the sisters. At first the pastoral team, composed of the sisters and one of the priests, would go to the landowners who would greet them politely and then fire off some firecrackers, which was the sign for the workers to come in from their shacks. There would be a makeshift arbor set up where the priest could say Mass, baptize the children, and perform marriages for couples who asked to have their union blessed. The sisters noticed that when the parents brought their children to be baptized, they called them their little "beasts." Both Dorothy and Joan wept when they heard them refer to their children like that.

The Catholic faith of the people was rooted in what they believed were three certainties: namely, you had to be baptized to be fully human; you had to go to Mass when you could, or you would go to hell; and living together before marriage was a sin. Apart from this, the majority of the people in the parish knew very little about church teachings. Certainly no awareness of Catholic social teaching had penetrated to these parts—whether among the poor workers or the wealthy landowners who co-existed in a semi-feudal relationship of domination and subservience.

By law, the peasant farmers were to give 10 percent of what they produced to the landowner, who always tried to demand 50 percent. The law also declared that whatever grew naturally in the forest could be harvested and sold by anyone. The landowner, however, would demand that the peasant farmers sell it to him for a fraction of the price they could get at the market. Most of the time, the workers had only vouchers to purchase what they needed from the land-owner. For the necessities of life, workers were completely dependent on the will of landowners who treated their work-ers as their "property," just as those before them had treated the workers as slaves.

During their first couple of months in Coroatá, the sis-ters divided up the town and went in twos to visit every single home. During the dry season, the sisters and priests worked in the town doing street preaching and watching for men who stood on the periphery of the crowd. Usually it was the women who would gather to listen. But gradually the men, who saw the women listening to the priest or sister, would move in closer to hear what was being said. Then, during the rainy season, the people were invited to attend a Bible study group taught by the priests. Most of those invited accepted the invitation and, little by little, they became more involved in the church and became leaders of their communities.

At the same time, the priests and sisters were working out-side the town. They had made the decision that they would go into the villages no longer by invitation of the landowners but by invitation of the people themselves. They would not stay in the landowner's house but with the peasant farmers. They wanted to show the people that their preference was to work with the poor. They would prepare the parents for their chil-dren's baptism and also prepare everyone present for the other sacraments. They would teach new hymns and lead the faithful in prayer, and they would begin to teach the members of the communities about their rights as human beings.

After taking note of those who could read a little and had some leadership ability, they would invite these potential leaders to become part of a team of people to gather their neighbors for prayer and worship when the priests or sisters were not available. In the base communities that emerged, the pastoral team had a chance to explain what it meant to live out the Gospel and to show that everyone's gifts have a place in the church. As Dorothy put it:

On weekends we used to go to the interior to any number of little villages. What we were trying to find were lay leaders. So, in every place we went to, we tried to find a few people who would say they were willing to help the community, to bring the people together, sing, have a Bible reading and reflection. They would be responsible for that. What we made sure of was that we went to no landowner's house. All the Masses and meetings were held at the leaders' homes. Another thing we did was to get to each village by the afternoon. We'd visit the homes and organize a meeting with the youth, women, and men. After the meeting of each of these groups, all the people would come together. Because they all had reflected on the same scriptural passage, we'd share. It was good, especially for the women, because at the community gatherings the only people who would ever talk were the men. The next day, the Mass would be based on the reflections of the previous night. The Mass was really a community celebration, based on how the people were living and what they were feeling about themselves.

How the people were living became painfully clear to Dorothy and the other sisters who saw the swollen bellies and stick legs of the children and heard of the brutality of the landowners' treatment of their workers. She and the other sisters knew that they had to help the people to learn about their rights. But it was not easy to change the attitudes of people who for centuries had lived in subservience. Gradually, the landowners became suspicious of the sisters, thinking they were "stirring up trouble" by pointing out the injustices that were so flagrant in the area.

The conflict between the church and the wealthy landowners erupted into the open when the two priests decided to put an end to the annual celebration of the patron's feast. It was the custom to have a novena of Masses for nine days before the feast of the patron saint of the area. But this had become one of the largest annual "money makers" for the landowners, who set up booths, gaming tables, and liquor stalls outside the church. Seeing how irreverent the feast had become, Fr. Lourenzo and Fr. Gabriel decided instead to say the nine novena Masses in the villages. The ranchers were furious and decided that they would have the procession in the town in spite of the priests. They set up their stalls and broke in the door of the church looking for the statue of Our Lady, which they intended to carry at the front of the procession. But their efforts were in vain. For some reason, they failed to find the statue, and the people would not participate in the procession as long as the priests and sisters were not among them.

On the feast of Pentecost, however, all the members of the base ecclesial communities in the interior were invited to Coroatá for a grand celebration. Hundreds of people came to attend a spirit-filled Mass followed by a procession. At each stop during the procession, they shared what they were doing in their village to make a stronger Christian community. This became an annual event. One year, the military sent plain-clothesmen to "infiltrate" the celebration and collect evidence of anti-government sentiments. The men arrived dressed in three-piece suits, which none of the villagers had, so they were rather conspicuous. They left after Sister Joan pointed her movie camera at each one of them, even though she didn't have any film.

As it turns out, Sister Dorothy and her fellow sisters had arrived at a critical time of transition in Brazil and for the church in Latin America. It had been two years since a military coup had taken place in 1964, initiating an era of violence and repression. In 1968, the bishops of Latin America held a conference in Medellín, Colombia, to apply the teachings of Vatican II to the situation of their continent. Examining not only the spread of military governments but also the underlying structures of social injustice, they named this situation as one of "institutionalized violence." The tenor of the conference marked a dramatic shift in the role of the church in Latin America. Whereas church leaders traditionally had understood their role as ministering to the spiritual needs of the people, the bishops at Medellín charged the church to take on a new role as a prophetic agent of evangelical justice and social transformation. In later years this would be defined as a "preferential option for the poor," a stance rooted in God's own love for the poor and oppressed.

Throughout Latin America the wealthy elite, who had always regarded the church as an ally in blessing the status quo, responded to the church's changing role with outrage and a sense of betrayal. Rumors spread among the wealthy that Communists had infiltrated the bishops' meeting. Those who stood by the poor in challenging injustice were seen no longer as religious workers but as dangerous subversives. In countries under military rule, to be named a subversive was to be marked for arrest, torture, and even death.

Despite the risks, the missionaries were determined to take up the challenge of Medellín. Dorothy grew even more convinced that her pastoral work involved helping the poor farmers to understand their rights and their dignity. In a letter of June 16, 1970, she wrote:

> You mentioned in closing that we, as Mary, have the mission of bringing Jesus to the world. When Sister Mary [Linscott] was here in May, I felt that was her mission, to see how we were going about our work to bring Christ to our people—to see if we were bringing the whole message of Christianity. I am sure that you are aware that there is a tendency when one is surrounded by misery to help man recognize his rights as a Son of God. This recognition leads him to a state of revolt. To help him see his obligations and responsibilities at the same time is harder, but so necessary if we are going to have a Christian leader.

Bishop Motta was always very supportive of the sisters' work in Coroatá. When he would come to visit, he would weep at seeing the children's suffering. He encouraged the priests and the sisters and expressed appreciation for their work. Once, as he was celebrating Mass for the community, he preached on the biblical story of Jezebel, the wife of King Ahab, who arranged to have a poor farmer killed because her husband wanted the man's vineyard (1 Kings 21:1–16). The bishop knew there were parallels in the stories of the people in the congregation. In his homily, he urged the people not to hate the wealthy, but to pray for them and for their conversion.

It was a lesson Dorothy would not forget. Afterwards, often, when she and her companions passed a rancher's house, they would say a prayer and sing songs of peace.

4

BLESSED ARE THE POOR

As the community of Sisters of Notre Dame developed in their understanding of the people of Coroatá and their needs, they began to adapt themselves to better serve the parishioners and the farmers. And yet their efforts occasionally caused confusion among some of the people. For example, the nuns did not wear a traditional habit like other sisters. First they had replaced their black skirts with gray ones made of lighter material. Next to go were the black stockings that had literally fallen apart. Sandals replaced oxfords. The changes left some people wondering whether these women were really sisters at all. And if the changes in garb weren't enough, the sisters received a donation of a jeep, which made them the only people in town besides the priests to drive a car. It was unheard of that women would drive a car in Coroatá at that time. Imagine—"nuns driving a car!"

By 1970, the Notre Dame community in Coroatá had changed. Sister Loretta Julia wanted all the sisters there to be from the same province. As a result, Sister Patricia McQuade went to São Domingos and Sister Barbara English left for São Luis. They were replaced by newcomers, Sisters Rebecca (Becky) Spires, Carol Clemens, and Jo Anne Depweg. However, three of the sisters, Carol, Jo Anne, and Joan, all came down with hepatitis. It took months for the three to recover and two of them had to return to the United States for treatment and recuperation. In the meantime, Dorothy wrote, while the other SNDs were recuperating, Lourenzo went to Italy for vacation. That left Gabe and myself in Coroatá. We had made all the rounds of the mission chapels in 1968 and some others in 1969. We had taken down the names of those interested in base communities, so we invited them to participate in a little course. That's when we thought of a parish center for formation. It was a new idea. The men would come in and spend a weekend together, and they began to get a sense of mission to their own people. They told each other what they were doing in their villages. They were getting a sense of group dynamics, and were getting better at reflection and the use of the Bible. The first session was so good that we had another one in two months, and then just kept having them.

At that time there was a Catholic Action group for youth, and they met at the center every month. When we went to the mission chapels, one of them would come with us and meet with the youth. The work was not just with adults. It was also with the youth in the interior.

At that time, too, a lot of strong questioning was happening about the landowners and how they dealt with the people. We studied about the rights of the rural workers on the land, and about what the landowners could not do. The people began to trust each other, and then they would share with each other the horrible things the landowners were doing to them. They began to ask, "What are we going to do about it?" And that's when things began to happen. By that time, the sick members of the team were well and back in Coroatá. Things were getting hot. The people were refusing to pay high land rentals. They wanted to sell their products in town and not to the landowner. They were becoming conscious of their rights.

On the evening of August 5, 1970, gunmen shot up the parish center in an effort to scare the village women who were with the nuns for a retreat. Also present were a number of village men whom the sisters had brought in with the aim of encouraging them to start a farm workers' union. When word arrived that gunmen were headed for the center, the sisters hid the men in the garage and then, in the early hours of the following morning, helped them get back safely to their villages.

This happened on the very evening that Sister Becky Spires arrived to join the community. Becky had heard about Dorothy, but did not know her well. One of her first impressions of Dorothy was when she saw her leave the center at around 10 PM after the shooting had stopped to go to the aid of a woman who had just given birth to her baby—ignoring the objections of the other sisters who feared for her safety. Becky recognized that this sister had extraordinary courage and an obvious love for the people.

There never was enough time for everything. After praying together each morning, Sister Dorothy and Fr. Gabriel would go to the outlying villages to form base ecclesial communities. Sister Joan formed youth groups in the town, taught religion and English in the schools, and accompanied Sister Dorothy to the interior villages on the weekends. Carol chose to work at the parish center, where she described her job as receptionist, janitor, secretary, and administrator. After a year, she assumed responsibility for the pastoral activities in one of the barrios where she was able to use all the training she had received from CENFI in developing base communities. Becky accompanied Dorothy on her rounds of the villages, and while Fr. Gabriel worked with the men, Dorothy worked with the women and Joan worked with the

youth. Sister Jo Anne coordinated the Family of God cate-
chetical groups with the training of people for the new roles
of the laity in the celebration of Mass.

On one occasion, Dorothy, Becky, and Fr. Gabriel were
working in one of the villages in the interior when a woman
asked for a ride back to the town, as she was ready to deliver
her baby. The pastoral team helped the woman into the jeep
and they set off. On the way, traveling over the bumpy roads,
she went into labor. Dorothy and Becky helped deliver a
healthy baby girl in the back of the jeep and arrived home
bloodied and pleased with themselves. The mother called the
baby "Maria Jeepie." It would not be the last time the sisters
would help deliver a baby in a remote area far from any
health facility.

The sisters also worked with prostitutes, young village
girls, many of whom had been sold by their parents or sent
away to make money for the family. They lived in the "*zona*"
district of Coroatá, the area where most of them plied their
trade. The sisters tried to teach them how to read and write,
as well as some basics about nutrition and health, and new
skills that would provide them with a means of livelihood.
Shortly after she arrived in the town, Dorothy wrote in a letter home to her mother: "Can use your prayers that God will
bless our efforts. We spent much time again last week visiting
with the prostitutes. There are so many of them here. They
welcome us warmly as we visit their shacks—all with dirt
floors—made of mud walls and palm branch roofs, but each
one has many little rooms with beds." Often, when the sisters
visited the prostitutes, it was the first time that these young
women felt as if they had some dignity and worth.

The leaders of the rural farmers were beginning to realize that there was strength in unity and that they could begin
to exercise some influence and thus not always be simply victims of the landowners. Almost all the land in Coroatá was
owned by seven families who responded to the farmers' ini-

tiatives by sending gunmen to threaten or assault them. The landowners would bribe the police and pay off the judge; they became a law unto themselves.

One of the instances that illustrated this was the time when the men from the small community of São Antonio decided to build a school for their children. By law, if any settlement had twenty-five or more children, it had the right to have a school; São Antonio had fifty children. Sister Dorothy had always encouraged the villagers to start a school if they didn't have one. She would help them find a teacher who often had no more than a primary grade education herself. Once the school began, Dorothy would go to the Department of Education and request for the teacher the salary that was guaranteed by law. She would also make sure that the teachers in the rural areas received teacher training and would organize the classes for them.

Sister Dorothy had encouraged the people of São Antonio to build their school. It was started by a group of fathers who had asked the landowner for permission to build the school on his land. He had refused, because he did not want the children to learn, especially about the fact that they had dignity and rights. But the men knew they had the law on their side and began to build the school anyway. Wearing just their shorts, since they were working in intense heat, they built a simple little building with a dirt floor and walls made of rough lumber. When they heard trucks coming, they instinctively knew something was wrong, so they urged their leader to leave and hide in the forest. Soon armed men appeared and, at gunpoint, forced the workers to tear down what they had built. They even made the men chop up the wood so it could never be used again. Then they loaded the men into the trucks and took them to jail.

When the wives heard what had happened, they gathered together some clothes for their husbands and walked the long distance into town. Someone ran ahead to inform the sisters.

They quickly collected food, gathered hammocks, and prepared a space where the women could stay that evening at the parish center.

Meantime, Sister Joan drove the car out to the road and waited. Soon the men's leader appeared. Joan hid him in the back of the car and took him to the convent, where he stayed for a few days until it was safe to get him back to his village.

Some of the sisters and the two priests set out for the jail. When they arrived, the police patted them down, looking for guns. One of the sisters said, "You're the ones with the guns. We don't have any."

Soon Fr. Gabriel arrived and demanded that the police release the men, who had done nothing illegal. The police chief responded by saying, "Get out or we will arrest you, too." The priest refused to leave, so the chief threw him into a cell.

When Dorothy saw all this, she and Fr. Lourenzo jumped into his jeep and sped toward São Luis right to the bishop's house. At that time, it was unheard of to put a priest in jail. The bishop returned with them and demanded that the police chief release the priest at once. The chief relented, but Fr. Gabriel refused to leave unless all the men were released as well. The police chief was furious, but he let them all go.

Tensions were mounting between the landowners and the police and anyone who was working for justice for the poor. The needs of the poor were simply ignored by the city officials who were working for the wealthy landowners. The mayor and the city officials did little to help the poor. On one occasion, the mayor took the gasoline meant for the city generator that provided lights for the school in the evening. He used the fuel for his own farm, leaving the students without classes for almost three months. Finally, some of the older children, in their frustration, painted light bulbs on several buildings with the words, "We want to study. Give us light."

Since Sister Joan worked for the schools and especially with the youth groups, the police chief called her in and threatened to put her in jail, even though she had had nothing to do with the protest. She responded by saying, "Well, I say okay. Fine. Let me go get my hammock and some books, but you have to promise me you won't let anyone bother me so I can get some rest." The police chief was totally frustrated, swore at her, and sent her home.

In June of 1971, Dorothy rejoiced in the visit of her mother, Edna. Mission life could be lonely, even with the support of the sisters and the love of the people. Dorothy very much missed contact with her family. When her mother arrived, Dorothy was thrilled to have her see what she was doing and to catch up on all the news of the family.

Edna had brought a microscope as a gift for the sisters, who began using it in their health care classes for women, especially in the villages. One of the ailments that afflicted everyone was intestinal worms. In fact, shortly after arriving in Coroatá, Dorothy wrote in a letter dated October 6, 1967:

> Father was over yesterday to tell us the result of his checkup at the doctors. Worms again!...We think it is the water we have to drink. You have to drink, as it is so hot here. We think we have worms too, as all of us are losing too much weight, so we are going to experiment with the worm medicine when we get home on Monday. Will let you know...It is a big joke here, as everyone from babies on up gets worms. So we are becoming more Brazilian each day.

In July, Dorothy and Becky took a course in midwifery from a young doctor who had come to help teach the people personal hygiene and sanitation. Even though many of the local women had been delivering babies, the doctor taught them better techniques. Infant mortality rates in Brazil were among the highest in the world at that time, and Dorothy and Becky wanted to respond to every kind of need the people had.

The community was growing in Coroatá. Two more Sisters of Notre Dame arrived to help with the pastoral team. Sister Jane Dwyer from Maryland and Sister Luci Ciccolini from Connecticut came after their course at CENFI and joined in the struggle for justice for the farm workers. There was also a succession of priests who came to serve the parish after the two Italian priests left to return to Italy. The base communities were taking on responsibility for the coordination and direction of their own leadership training and Bible study, as well as conducting Sunday services in the absence of a priest. In fact, some of the leaders in the villages had their wives make cassocks for them, until the sisters explained that they didn't need to wear cassocks in order to hold prayer services on Sundays.

Exploring the Bible together and taking scripture courses given by the sisters and priests inevitably led the farmers to questions about their rights to the land. This led to further study of the land statutes in Brazilian law. Dorothy always believed that the law would be upheld by the authorities. Sometimes she would be reduced to tears when she realized that the authorities often circumvented or ignored the law. What hurt most of all was to think that those who could help the poor simply did not care to do so. But the pastoral teams were making some progress in the town and the sisters were seeing the fruits of their labors.

While some of the other sisters chose to move on to other works, Dorothy and Joan stayed on. In 1974, both sisters were given the "Honorary Citizen Award" of Coroatá. They were very honored and pleased, but made it quite clear that they would not go to the city hall to receive the award unless representatives of the poor farmers could go to the ceremony. On the day the award was bestowed on the sisters, the base community leaders were allowed into the city hall to witness the ceremony. They had never been permitted to enter the building before. Clutching their straw hats and dressed in their shabby clothes, the farmers were given the front seats so they could see this honor bestowed on the sisters they had come to love. It was a joyous day for everyone and a sign that things were starting to change, at least in some small ways.

Priests and religious all over Brazil were beginning to feel the pressure of the military repression of anyone who questioned the government. Any person helping the poor was liable to be considered a Communist. Even the encyclical of Pope Paul VI, *Populorum Progressio*, which dealt with the injustice of poverty and the widening gulf between the rich countries of the world and the poor, was considered a Communist document. The sisters heard of the arrest of two priests in nearby parishes. Fr. Antonio José, a Brazilian priest, and Fr. Xavier, a Canadian priest (and now a bishop of Maranhão), were from the nearby parishes of São Benedicto de Rio Preto and Urbano Fantes. They were accused of establishing base communities and starting communal farming projects. The landowners claimed that the priests were instigating terror and were actually Communists trying to infiltrate the country. Fr. Antonio José, because he was a Brazilian, was severely tortured by a policeman with whom he had grown up and who had been a classmate of his in the seminary. Fr. Xavier was not physically tortured, but he went on a fast in protest of the torture of his friend. When Fr. Antonio José was brought to trial, he showed the marks of having been hung by his wrists and ankles "like a pig."

The bishop had asked all the sisters to be present at the trial, so the Sisters of Notre Dame from Coroatá, São Domingos, and São Luis went to Fortaleza, spent a day in prayer, and appeared in the courtroom for the proceedings. When the lawyer asked the accusing landowner what the priests were doing, he replied, "They are telling people they should love one another." At this, some of the people in the courtroom burst out laughing. The judge dismissed the case.

Shortly afterwards, there was a military takeover in Coroatá. A military police officer came to the house with an

issue of *Time* magazine that contained an article about the
torture of people in Brazil, citing the case of Fr. Antonio José
among others. Sister Jo Anne Depweg was the only one at
home when he came to the convent and showed her the magazine, saying, "You know it is all a lie." Sister Jo Anne told
him that she was at the trial and had seen the marks on Fr.
Jose's wrists. The man left. However, he came back to the
house several times, proudly showing off his certificates from
the School of the Americas.

The farmers were gradually growing in strength and con-
viction. Dorothy had worked very hard to convince them that
they could organize a farmers' union and work together to
bring about change. When she returned to the United States
occasionally on her home visits, she saw the success of Cesar
Chavez's work and the rise of the United Farm Workers
Union. She saw how they achieved better housing, increased
wages, health care, and legal rights. Her dream was to see the
Brazilian farm workers achieve similar benefits. She had already seen how they had begun to feel their power even in the
midst of the many threats of violence against them. Although
she often wished for more support from the clergy, especially
the bishops, there *was* a Bishops' Pastoral Plan that encouraged the formation of unions among the workers and she felt
empowered by that. Given the tenor of the times, with the
implementation of the teachings of the Second Vatican Council, the Medellín documents, and the Bible itself, Dorothy felt
confident that the truth was on her side, and that every person
had a right to a dignified life, without constant fear of the police, the landowners, or the military.

She rejoiced in the fact that the leaders whom she had
mentored were taking their place in the formation of the
Farmers' Union in the Coroatá region. It was well under way
and she was proud of their leadership. Even when warned by
her own sisters about "getting into trouble," she seemed to
feel even more strongly that she was called to minister to the
poor, to help them feel empowered, and to urge them to

work together; especially in the rural areas of Brazil. That is why, when the Transamazon Highway opened up in the early 1970s, she felt a need to accompany those who went in search of land and freedom from slavery.

Dorothy sensed that she had done all she could for Coroatá and it was time to move on. At their assembly held in July 1974, the Sisters of Notre Dame in Brazil discussed going into a new region in the interior. Not all were in favor of this. Some argued that there were few enough Sisters of Notre Dame in Brazil; they feared that too much dispersion would isolate them from one another. But, most of all, they worried that Dorothy and Becky, who also wished to go, would be moving into a political "hot spot" that could trigger implications for the Sisters of Notre Dame anywhere in Brazil.

Dorothy, who was not easily dissuaded, countered the arguments against moving deeper into the Amazon with her own arguments. The diocese of Marabá in the state of Pará, she pointed out, had very few religious and priests ministering there, whereas the diocese of São Luis in Maranhão already had a number of Sisters of Notre Dame. She was impressed that the diocese of Marabá had declared a dedication to the poor, which resonated with her own desires. Furthermore, it was an area that was attracting migrants from other regions, individuals and families responding to the government's promise of land for poor people willing to settle along the Transamazon Highway. She pleaded, "We can accompany our people." After much discussion, the sisters decided that Dorothy and Becky should constitute an "ad hoc" committee to investigate the possibility of starting a new mission in Pará.

Dorothy had been to Rio de Janeiro to study the Brazilian Agrarian Reform Movement as well as the challenges of farming in the Amazon region. While she was there, she had met Bishop Estevão from Marabá who had sought her out and presented her with a proposal for Sisters of Notre Dame to come to his diocese. In August of 1974 Dorothy and Becky visited the diocese of Marabá, where they saw the house that the church had already prepared for them and met Fr. Mario Hoss, who would be working with them once in a while. During the visit, the two sisters assisted in a meeting of the pastoral agents. It was a very good experience for all. The bishop, the priests, the religious, and the laity all worked on an equal footing to find a better way to serve the people who were suffering so much. Working this way was something the sisters had not experienced in Maranhão, and they felt real hope for the future here. The people in the diocese of Marabá were awaiting their arrival with great anticipation. Actually, this worried the two sisters, because there had been no firm decision by the Sisters of Notre Dame as to whether they could actually go to Marabá. However, Dorothy and Becky clearly felt that this was a place for Notre Dame, and they decided to offer themselves to be missioned there.

In September of 1974, the Sisters of Notre Dame in Brazil held an extraordinary assembly where Dorothy and Becky presented their proposal and a rationale for sending them to a new region. Fr. Mario Hoss also spoke on their behalf to the group. Eventually, and despite their grave reservations, the sisters reluctantly agreed to have the two nuns go to Marabá in the state of Pará. Dorothy would go right away and Becky would go after finishing her course on the Rural Pastoral in Bahia.

Prior to Dorothy's leaving for Pará, the base communities in Coroatá missioned her to her new endeavor. She described the experience:

> The people felt they were missioning me to carry to other Maranhenses what we had done in Coroatá. When I first came to Coroatá, I didn't know anything about the work. The people didn't either. We all learned together how to walk the road of liberation. It was a great night when they missioned me. The idea

was that we would walk together in this new land with this new people, and I would carry with me the spirit of Coroatá.

The two sisters were eager to set out on their new mission. Dorothy traveled to the city of Marabá and explained to the bishop that she and Becky wanted to move deeper into the forest and work with the poor there.

The bishop gave them permission to do this. He added that, if they would commit to a minimum of three years of service to the area, the diocese would support them financially with a stipend of CR$400 (about $200) each per month.

Dorothy and Becky would be moving into an area near the Transamazon Highway that was drawing people from many different areas of Brazil. Once there, the sisters would be facing the challenge of trying to bring together people of different ethnic backgrounds, dialects, and experiences. The seat of the municipality was far away and the civil authorities had little interest in and paid no attention to what was happening in this remote area. It would be a very different experience from the one they had known in Coroatá.

5
DEEPER INTO THE FOREST

Brazil was the only Latin-American country to intervene on behalf of the Allied Forces in World War II. As a result the country was rewarded with much needed aid from the World Bank and the Inter-American Development Bank. During the 1960s and 1970s, Brazil implemented a program to use the loan money to develop the Amazon region for cattle raising, mining, and logging. Conflicts and disputes arose regarding the use of the land generously parceled out by the government to the wealthy. Part of the deal was an economic agreement between Brazil and the United States favoring multinational companies. In this climate, poor farmers never had a chance, as rich landowners moved aggressively to buy false titles to state land and to acquire huge tracts for agribusiness or as a bargaining chip for some possible future enterprise.

Ranching had begun in Brazil with the Portuguese colonization, and from that time there had been a history of *latifundia*, the granting of immense areas of land to a few wealthy Portuguese families who were favored by the government regardless of any people, such as the indigenous tribes, who might be living there. In 1962, for example, the state had entitled 250,000 acres of land in southern Pará for the Santa Teresa *latifundia* alone. It became symbolic of the expectation of the wealthy for similar grants when the government opened huge tracts of land for settlement along the Transamazon Highway. The government saw these enterprises as a way of generating the income it needed to pay back its loans. In order to increase Brazilian exports, the government subsidized ranching through SUDAM (Superintendency for the Development of the Amazon), an organization that approved the establishment of ranches averaging sixty thousand acres each. The plan for economic growth was called the "Brazilian Miracle," but it soon became known by the poor as "Savage Capitalism," since it inevitably exploited the land and the people in the name of development. According to the government's propaganda, the enterprises would provide employment for the landless. However, once the land was cleared of the trees, burned, and planted with cattle grass, the workers were fired, since only a few were needed as ranch hands. Built into the process of opening the Amazon region for settlement was the opportunity for profiteering and the inevitable conflict between the landowners and the poor.

The settlement programs for the landless were coordinated by the Institute of Colonization and Agrarian Reform (INCRA), which soon proved ineffective and disorganized. Charged with the duty of helping poor farmers establish themselves on 250 acres of land in the territory opened up by the government for the development of the Amazon region, in most cases INCRA neglected to give the poor legal title to their land. They sometimes put them on land claimed by the wealthy, who often used fraudulent claims, known as *grilagem*,* forged documents made up to look as if they dated back to the time of the Portuguese rule, to expel the poor farmers. If the farmers resisted, they were beaten, burned out, or killed by

---

*The process of obtaining land illegally and often forcefully. From the Portuguese word for "cricket," since it describes the method used to forge documents by putting them into boxes with crickets so that the secretions of the insects would color the paper to make it look old. Sometimes the documents themselves revealed the fraud, since the landowner would sign the paper with a ballpoint pen not available in the 1800s.

gunmen hired by the landowners. Indigenous tribes were often the target of the worst brutality. They would be driven off their tribal lands by ranchers and loggers and forced to flee farther and farther into the Amazon forest. Often the farmers followed them, hoping to escape from the landowners.

Believing that the government would protect them and that they were being offered an opportunity to have their own land to provide for their families, thousands of landless poor flocked to the Amazon in search of a new life. Most did not even know that they needed a written document to prove their right of ownership. Land sharks and sophisticated people from the south of Brazil, hoping to cash in on the possibility of grabbing land and then selling it to the large ranchers or loggers, took advantage of the uneducated farmers and demanded that they leave their farms, threatening them with guns if they resisted. At times, the ranchers or loggers would offer the poor farmers a minimal amount of cash for their land. For some, it was more money than they had ever seen in their lives. Threatened with violence if they did not sell, they would accept the money and go to the cities. Once there, they learned how little they had in relation to the expenses they faced. Often they would end up living in the *favelas*, the slum areas that are so prominent today in Brazil. It was very difficult to find employment in the cities and many people ended up begging just to stay alive.

Meanwhile, the government was putting out massive propaganda about the advantages poor people would have in helping Brazil extend its frontiers by moving into the Transamazon region. For people who had spent their whole lives in slave labor to rich landowners, this was seen as an invitation to become independent and gain title to state land. They came in droves from all over Brazil, clearing the land and beginning a new life in the state of Pará.

In September 1974 Dorothy went to Abel Figueiredo, which was ninety kilometers from the city of Marabá. By the time Becky arrived in November, Dorothy and Fr. Hoss had

already been visiting the principal villages in the area to set up
base ecclesial communities. Dorothy wrote:

> The people were very willing to work in community,
> because they were all alone. Many had former experi-
> ence with base communities in another reality. Now
> the experience was of people from different cultures
> trying to come together and build a new Church—a
> community. We were hardly getting started when the
> land sharks showed up. They began to pressure the
> people, saying that they, the land sharks, had title
> from way back to huge tracts of land. The situation
> became bloody. Homes were burnt. The police were
> paid to scare the people with machine guns. They
> would surround their homes and force the people out.

It was hard for Dorothy and Becky to watch what was
happening. By the time they moved to Abel Figueiredo, forty
million acres of the Brazilian rain forest had disappeared.
With the continuing clearing and burning of the land for cattle ranching and logging, hundreds of thousands of acres of
virgin forest were being destroyed each year. Fr. Mario Hoss
joined Dorothy and Becky on their pastoral team as all three
visited the settlements and heard the stories of repression and
violence. One of the factors that made building community
difficult was the presence of the military, which had been sent
to Pará to destroy the small bands of guerillas in the forest.
The military convinced people that those groups were made
up of criminals, thieves, and outlaws. Some who had helped
the "people in the forest" grew fearful and offered to be
guides to the military, who sought out and "eliminated" the
Communists. Others were accused of aiding the forest people
and were summarily arrested, beaten, and tortured by the
military. Any group that gathered for the purpose of dis-
cussing change came under suspicion. As a consequence, the
development of base communities also became increasingly

dangerous. The military was all too anxious to prove that these groups were subversive.

Dorothy and Becky heard of the expulsion of four hundred families from their cultivated land by one of the multinational companies in the area. The gross injustices infuriated the pastoral team. They collected maps, tables, and reports, all signed by the people. In the face of that crisis, many people contributed money to allow Bishop Estevão and two others to go to Brasilia to ask for federal help. The group was well received, but nothing was resolved. The ranchers, loggers, and land sharks paid off the local police and, in some cases, the judges, so that the poor rarely, if ever, got any support from the civil authorities. It was obvious, however, that the church was on the side of the poor.

It was also clear that the poor farmers knew very little about their rights. Dorothy became part of the MEB (Movement for Basic Education) Team, which had been set up to promote adult literacy. She and Becky obtained small, inexpensive Bibles, which they sold to the people for a nominal amount. As soon as the adults began to read, they absorbed the teachings of the Bible, which they applied to their own situation. Stories like that of the exodus were particularly meaningful for them.

Besides the problems with the attempts to rob the people of their land, there were conflicts between the group from Maranhão and the people of the south. Dorothy described the problem: "The people from the south had know-how on making a family farm self-sufficient, and they came up with money. The Maranhenses arrived with only hoes and shovels. They had no financial security. They were hungry most of the time. Many of them came alone and so had no family support. They ended up selling their land and working for the new landowners." The people from the south saw the Maranhenses as lazy and ignorant, Dorothy wrote, "so we were happy to be able to defend them and help the folks from the south understand the Maranhenses."

As more and more people moved into the area, the diocese was split into two parts. A new bishop, Dom Alano, arrived to take over the northern section. This was also a period when efforts were made to find excuses for getting rid of the priests and sisters. Several foreign priests who were working for the poor were deported.

One time, while Dorothy and Becky were holding a retreat for some of the women from the interior, all foreign religious were called in by the military. Dorothy quickly went back to the house to collect anything—like books or documents—that could be used against them. She put everything in a plastic bag and took it to a neighbor who buried it in her back yard.

Bishop Alano insisted on going to the inquest with the religious. "Ladies first," the military lieutenant said as he welcomed them in perfect English. He then pulled out song sheets and handouts from a pile of papers that the sisters had used for eucharistic celebrations and classes. One was a copy of the United Nations' Universal Declaration of Human Rights. The lieutenant accused Dorothy and Becky of sowing dissension by using the declaration, which he called subversive.

Eventually they were all released, and they concluded that it had just been a scare tactic and a warning. However, at about the same time, they heard of a Brazilian priest who had been tortured psychologically. His tormentor, another proud graduate of the School of the Americas, told the priest that although he had not destroyed his body, he had destroyed his soul, and that if he did not do whatever he was told, his mother and his sister would be killed. The priest took his own life. It was a time of rampant terror.

The Brazilian bishops, responding to the rising violence, established the Pastoral Land Commission (CPT) to proclaim once again the rights of the poor. Dorothy and Becky enthusiastically told the people about the bishops' teaching, which further encouraged the people's hope of finding justice. Fr. Mario Hoss eventually moved in to live with the sisters and they formed a strong community bond. They prayed together, planned and evaluated their work together, and regularly visited the base communities.

Transportation was always a problem. Dorothy and Becky's Volkswagen often sank in the deep mud and had to be literally lifted out by several men; the roads were perilous at best. Even though they had a car, they would spend long hours walking along thin paths through the forest to reach the settlers. The team reached out to the farmers, bringing them together for Bible study and Mass and encouraging them to help each other. All of this enabled the people to be stronger and more resistant in the face of oppression.

By 1976, it had become evident that there was a need for a place to meet. With help from a foundation in Germany, the pastoral team built a chapel/community center. There they held a series of reflections on salvation history for representatives from the twenty base communities that they had established. The meetings would take place every weekend on a rotating basis: one weekend with the men, the next with the women, and the one after that with the young people. It was a time of growth and a great spirit was developing among the people. When Fr. Mario's five-year contract ended, he returned to Rio Grande and an Italian priest, Fr. Maboni, came as pastor.

Trouble started in a neighboring parish where another Italian priest was being threatened by an American family who claimed ownership of sixty-six thousand hectares of land. About three thousand Brazilians lived on the land, some near the border of the sisters' parish. Dorothy and Becky encouraged the people in their resistance and reflected with them about their rights. Eventually the conflict led to violence. About thirty Brazilians were arrested and the priest was expelled from the country. The incident made the people grow fearful; they never knew when they might be driven from their own farms.

The new pastor in Abel Figueiredo, Fr. Maboni, was unfamiliar with the troubles in Pará and felt very threatened by them. He soon asked his bishop for a change, and was transferred to the southern part of the new diocese. Just before he left, the bishop asked Fr. Fontanella, who was serving in a neighboring parish, to carry a letter of support to a group of farmers in a land dispute. The bishop felt that the priest would be safe. However, the police arrested, tortured, and jailed him, accusing him of subversion. The police also forced him into saying that Dorothy and Becky were at the head of a growing subversive movement. Even before this, Dorothy's name had appeared on a police list of suspected Communists.

When Dorothy and Becky visited Fr. Fontanella in the hospital where he was recovering after being released from jail, he asked for their forgiveness, which they readily offered. As soon as he could travel, he was sent back to Italy. Even Fr. Maboni, when he reached his new parish in the southern diocese, was arrested and tortured. Arrest could be sudden and unexpected; just being a priest was dangerous.

After these episodes, the diocese stopped keeping records of activities for fear of the police investigating and persecuting the people. As a consequence, there was a drop in the numbers of people participating in the activities of the base communities. Fear gripped the people. Dorothy wrote:

> The situation continued in conflict. More rich came into the area and kept taking over huge tracts of land. The people couldn't hold onto the land. There was no recourse to justice when they resisted, and the police were paid to violate the rights of those who stood up for their rights. Little by little, they moved farther and farther into the virgin forest. The little communities we had worked with began to dwindle. People were on the move again for survival. And survival meant finding land to farm and space to live.

When no priest came after Fr. Maboni's departure, the people began to take on more responsibilities. Afraid that

Dorothy and Becky would be expelled as well, they accelerated the process of sharing responsibility for parish duties. The two sisters had permission to baptize, perform marriages, distribute Communion, conduct community penance services, and anoint the sick and the dying. Occasionally a priest would come to say Mass for the community.

Once again, the sisters were summoned to Army headquarters for questioning. They did not tell the people they were being summoned because they did not want to cause them alarm. However, they found out later that the people had kept a prayer vigil for them until they returned. When they did return, the people made them promise that they would be notified anytime Dorothy and Becky were traveling out of the area so they would not worry about them.

By 1977, the government was building another highway, this one cutting right through the area to which many of the people had migrated. Once again, the government took advantage of the rural farmers who had cleared and opened the forest and who had suffered from all the terrible diseases they had contracted in the process. Malaria was a common ailment and Dorothy had her share of it as well. She wrote:

> Becky and I began to accompany these people, many of whom we already knew. It was a marvelous thing because we already had their confidence. They welcomed us with open arms to help them get together with other people who had moved into the area and to get started with base communities. They were born overnight, survival communities, you might say.

By the end of the year, there were thirty communities along the new road. But the land sharks were coming as fast as the road was being built, and the sisters felt they needed to establish support systems for the farmers.

It was a battle right from the start. For two years, the sisters followed a pattern of going into the woods one weekend and the next having a three-day rotating course for men, women, and the young people. When the sisters went into the woods, they would stay with any family that would have them and eat whatever the family had to offer, mostly rice and beans. Occasionally, the farmer would have hunted a monkey or an armadillo or brought back a fish from a stream, but these treats were very rare.

In November 1978, Beta, a university student from Belém, offered to come to live with the sisters and help them. The next year two seminarians, Colemar and Eduardo, and a young woman, Carminha, came. In addition, Fr. Humberto, who came with them, offered to give steady help to the team, and Sister Eliska, another Sister of Notre Dame, offered to come part time. With this new help, Dorothy and Becky decided to form two teams. Becky, Beta, Colemar, Carminha, and Sister Eliska would compose one team and stay in Figueiredo; Dorothy, Eduardo, and Fr. Humberto would form the other team farther along the road on PA150*. Eventually, the two teams worked independently.

By the next year, Dorothy and her team had moved to a town called Arraia. Dorothy described the living conditions: "We lived with a family, Manoel and Maria and their three little boys. They opened their home to us and gave us everything we needed. We moved in and out, up and down the road, and whenever we came back, we had a home. It was a fantastic thing they did for us."

However, the land situation was getting worse. The land sharks had the military police working for them and were paying them off. Twelve people had been killed by the police in just two years and nothing had been done about it. The bishop used every kind of communication to get the word out about what was happening in the area and tried to get support for the people. INCRA, the government organ for land reform, was declared incompetent. Some of its members

---

*PA designates locations on the Pan American Highway.

feared for their lives and therefore remained silent about the abuses.

Then GETAT* was created. This was a federal group with the last word on land conflicts. In addition, there was a state organ for control of the land. Both organizations were irritated by the presence of the sisters, priests, and laywomen, seeing them as responsible for the people's resistance to those trying to take their land. They put out a warrant for the arrest of Dorothy and Becky. The sisters, however, having been secretly informed of the attempt to arrest them, traveled to Belém to seek legal help. They went to the state organization and declared their rights. The organization's leader was able to rescind the order for their arrest, but warned the sisters that if they ever had a meeting on land issues, they would be picked up. After that, they became much more careful; they did not want to appear to be leaders, since it was the people's struggle.

In the beginning of 1979, Dorothy returned to the United States for a home visit. Such visits offered an opportunity, among other things, to receive medical treatment for worm infestation, or whatever other malady she was suffering at the time. But the sisters in the States always found her cheerful and happy, ready to listen to any who approached her and ready for a good time. She loved a party, especially if ice cream was on the menu. When she visited one of her siblings, she would enjoy watching a Cincinnati Bengals football game and having a beer with everyone as they cheered on the team. Still, while she clearly had a good time, it was obvious that "her people" were still on her mind and she was anxious to get back to them.

During her home visits, she entered into the many discussions that were going on in the seventies and eighties re-

---

*Grupo Executivo de Terras do Araguaia-Tocatins, Executive Group for the Araguaia-Tocatins. An organization established by the military regime to deal with land conflicts and titling in the Amazon frontier area.

garding the changes in religious life. One of the ways the Sisters of Notre Dame began addressing some of the social justice issues of the time was to invite all the sisters of the province to sign a corporate statement about such things as nuclear disarmament or opposition to the death penalty. One of these issues was particularly important to Dorothy. It was a statement of support for the "Sanctuary Movement," which defied the government by welcoming political refugees, especially from Central America, who were escaping the oppression and terror in their countries.

A letter Dorothy wrote from Brazil on January 8, 1981, points to the contrast between what she observed in her home visits and the situation she was experiencing in Brazil:

> Dear Sisters,
> I don't know where to start, as my head swims with terrible happenings. First, I'd like to wish you all a very happy '81. What does happy '81 mean? And for whom?
>
> In June I wrote a long letter to the province about our reality and I have a feeling that it never arrived as no reference was ever made to it. It was about the death of a farm peasant murdered by a carefully planned plot to scare the poor into a more crushing oppression.
>
> I'm writing again from a bit of a hideaway, as a peasant in one of the twenty-five villages that we care for was murdered Friday, the 2nd of January. He was murdered in front of his little shack because he is one who has taken an active part in resisting the crushing power of the rich landowners in our area. In this village the same gunman murdered a peasant father of ten small children in March of '80 and paralyzed another with a bullet in the spine in December of '79. He has threatened some seven or eight more and no one knows the day or place that this paid gunman will strike.

In February of '80 the peasants of our region organized a class labor union, a little at a time preparing organized resistance. They are becoming stronger and more courageous as each act of brutality strikes one of them. Our main village where the priest, a layman, and I have a little house, is the center of constant conflict. The population here is about 18,000 and 95% are peasant farmers trying to plant on an area with what you might call squatter rights. The rich, backed by easily acquired funds from international banks and farm projects, use all means to rob the people of their small survival plots, as in a capitalistic system the poor have no reason to have land since financially it is not viable. Surrounding the village are some twenty-five smaller communities and all belong to this newly organized group to defend the rights of the peasant farmer.

When our brother Jose was murdered Friday night, a group came to our town to tell of the brutality and ask for help. Being 11:00 at night, and only I at home, we tried to make plans. They went back to their village the same night, as their families were afraid. The next day I hunted for a pick-up truck to bring the body to our town, as a murder has to be reported. Only the better-off have cars, but I did find a man who lent me his pick-up and I went to bring the body. Two tires blew on the return. You can imagine. These are a few of the details and the rest I leave to your imagination.

Since that day, the poor are planning more vigorous means of self-defense, as the authorities never take any stand so as not to offend those who support the system. Most of the planning has taken place in our little home, which is in the middle of the village. Our house is constantly watched, so the constant coming and going of the peasants from many villages day and night was becoming dangerous, as we have federal police as plainclothes men constantly observing in the name of national security. In the wee hours of the feast of the Three Kings, it was decided that I should get out for a few days as the new law against foreigners is an open door to get rid of anyone who disturbs the false peace. Therefore, I'm at this small farm house on the edge of town.

The attitude of the peasants is from Isaiah 9, where he says that the rod that oppressively rules is to be broken, and chapter 58—What is the sacrifice that God asks of us? Also, Luke 4, where Christ tells of his mission, as well as the command to expel all evil from this world. The attitude right now is to take justice into their own hands in the name of God.

While here in this little hideaway, I'm reading *News and Views* and *Speak-Up* of Christmas, '80, and *Forum** where corporate response is being debated. My response is that if we are really involved—heart, mind, and soul—with the poor oppressed by the system there is no doubt about what we must do to give a corporate response. We can't talk about the poor. We must be poor with the poor, and then there is no doubt as to how to act. If we strip ourselves of all our extras that consume so much of our time and thoughts on how to care for them, our leftover time is colored and it is hard not to give a radical Gospel response.

I feel this way as I see thousands and thousands of people dying inch by inch under the capitalistic system that we know is diabolical, but somehow we fear to point it out. Sister Sandra Price in her article

News and Views, *Speak-Up*, and *Forum* are publications of the Ohio Province.

on El Salvador says it well, as also Sr. Mary Evelyn in *News and Views*.

We as a congregation consecrated to announce the Gospel can't waste time trying to convince ourselves as ND what our response should be. Golly, did we make our life so comfortable and withdrawn from reality that we can't see the social sins that our keeping silence is supporting? It's good that we're at least trying to wake ourselves up as a group, to be more of a prophetic response. But instead of spending so much time on waking ourselves up, let's spend our energies getting with it.

Those who dedicated themselves and somewhere along the line chose a more secure easy way out may be seeing the others really involved, as the Gospel asks of us. The grace of conversion will come. No time to waste—the poor are being crushed as we debate the issue.

She signed the letter, "Love you all much." The sisters in Ohio had been warned to be careful about what they wrote to Dorothy. No one knew to what degree her actions and words were being monitored. All knew, however, that Dorothy was in dangerous territory and that her heart ached at what she saw happening all around her.

By 1979, Becky had decided to stay in Abel Figueiredo and work full time for the Indian tribes served by CIMI, the Bishop's Missionary Indians Council. Dorothy, Fr. Humberto, and Eduardo were in Arraia, which was later called Jacunda. Eventually, they built a parish house in the town. The pastoral team continued to give solace and heart to the people who were facing even more obstacles.

At the invitation of the Brazilian government, more and more multinationals were moving in. This made it even more profitable for the land sharks to throw people off the land. Profiteers could get high prices for the land when they sold it to the multinationals, who were not interested in buying land that had people living on it. Gunmen were very easy to find. They would bring back the ear or the tongue of the person they had killed and collect their fee from the land shark. Volkswagen, Mercedes-Benz, Phillips, and Pão de Acucar were some of the multinationals that moved in. One government project, Electra Notre, involved a proposal to build a huge dam that would provide energy for the large industries interested in going to Brazil. A new industrial park was to be constructed near Belém and it would need to be supplied with electric power. Taking the rural farmers off the land was one way of providing the cheap labor needed to build the dam.

In carrying out preliminary research on minerals in the Marabá region, U.S. Steel had discovered what was considered the richest iron deposit in the world. The company now had big plans for the area. The people went to Belém to protest, but they were pushed off the land in spite of the promises of the government there to the contrary.

It was always the same story. The authorities would allow the farmers to stay on the land for about five years and work hard to clear it. Then the farmers would be forced off to make way for roads and large business enterprises. All the government could see was a way of bringing business into the country and all it cared about was paying off debts and placating the wealthy.

Dorothy still held out hope for the people and rejoiced in small triumphs. She wrote, "Our work with the people continued to animate their faith and hope in themselves, helped them to understand their rights, and motivated them to organize."

In 1982, the area of Jacunda was proclaimed a municipality. It had a population of twenty-four thousand. By that time, the people were so well organized that they were able to get three councilmen from the base communities elected to the municipal council. The son of a farm worker became mayor. All these things were signs of growth in self-confidence and organization.

Dorothy was thrilled and grateful for any signs of hope for her people. What she may not have fully appreciated was that the people saw *her* as their real sign of hope. She believed in them and respected them. No one had ever felt that way about them before, and they loved her for it.

The Stang family. (Dorothy, first row, far right)

Dorothy in Julienne
High School, age 16.

Dorothy, known as Sister Mary
Joachim, in religious habit,
c. 1950s.

Dorothy outside the sister's house
in Coroatá, Brazil, 1968.

Farmers claiming plots along the Transamazon Highway.

Dorothy and co-workers educating on problems
with a proposed dam on the Xinhu River.

A new settlement in Amazon Forest, early 1990s.

Dorothy explaining land rights to
government officials.

Amazon settlement.

6

ON THE TRANSAMAZON

An American woman, dressed in a tee shirt and jeans, "stirring up" the rural farmers and claiming to be a Catholic nun, was enough to frighten even some of the pastoral workers. They had never seen anyone like Sister Dorothy Stang before. Often she would share her frustrations with a friend and be reduced to tears as she spoke of how she was treated, not only by government officials but even by some of the clergy who disagreed with her passion for social justice.

If she was anything, she was forthright. She would boldly go to the federal offices and voice her complaints about the treatment of the farm workers who had been promised land and were being driven off by the ranchers and loggers. She had carefully studied the law and she did not hesitate to remind government officials of what it said. If they refused to see her, she would sit outside their offices for hours, waiting for them to give her some time. Once, when an official said he had not received one of her three letters of protest, she insisted on seeing his files and easily found a copy of the "missing" letter. She constantly sensed she was being lied to, betrayed, and treated with condescension. She often felt like a voice crying out in the wilderness, trying to let people know about the suffering and injustice that were taking place, aware that those who were in a position to help really did not care.

Even when talking to some of the priests it was difficult at times to feel as if she were being taken seriously, so threatened were they by the assertiveness of the emerging base communities and their desire to participate in the affairs of the church. In addition, the culture of "machismo" made it difficult for government officials and certain members of the clergy to accept the leadership of an outspoken woman. Some of them worried that Dorothy was "out of control." After a number of priests had been killed or expelled from the country and Dorothy's name appeared on a "hit list" published in the press, even Bishop Alano began to get nervous about her actions. Feeling that the bishop had lost confidence in her, Dorothy believed that it was better for her to move on.

By 1982, Dorothy felt that she wanted to go even deeper into the forest, following the settlers who were moving there after having been driven off the land they had previously occupied. She went to Altamira on the Xingu River to talk to Bishop Erwin Krautler, telling him of her desire to work with the "poorest of the poor." Although the bishop may have had some misgivings about this woman, he was struck by the stories of the work she had done in Abel Figueiredo and Jacunda and assured her that if she were looking for the poor in the most abandoned places, he could definitely provide her that opportunity.

The bishop told Dorothy that the settlers on the east side of the Transamazon Highway had nothing, that their condition was desperate. He was very open about the difficulty of even finding the settlers who had gone deep into the forest. When Dorothy told the bishop that this was just what she wanted to do, he welcomed her into his prelature. She was invited to stay with the Precious Blood Sisters who had a high school right across the road from the bishop's house.

Although she had a small motorbike given to her by St. Rita's Parish in Dayton, Ohio, it did not prove strong enough to handle the roads out to Anapu. Sometimes she would wait five or six hours before hitching a ride with a truck going in that direction. In the dry season the bus from Altamira toward the settlements passed only once a day. In the wet season it often could not navigate the treacherous road at all. Once she reached an area where people were living, she would have to walk for hours to find them deep in the forest. When she finally reached the settlers, she would ask if she might stay the night with one of the families, as she could not return the same day. After seeing how much there was to be done among these isolated farmers, she realized that she could not keep on spending most of her time just trying to reach them. There were no schools, no health care facilities, and only occasionally, when Fr. Lucas, a missionary priest, would come, was there access to Mass (for which some people walked as far as thirty kilometers). There were thousands of people in the area at that time, some of them squatters who were not too anxious for anyone to find them.

Finally, Fr. Lucas asked if there was a family that would be willing to have Sister Dorothy live with them for awhile. At first, the request was met with silence. The poor settlers lived in shacks with dirt floors, no running water, and no electricity. They barely had enough to eat themselves and wondered why this American nun would ever want to share their poverty with them. Eventually, Doña Antonia Barbosa and her husband, Dio, offered to allow Dorothy to move into the little shack where they lived with their ten children. A few days later, Dorothy arrived at their door carrying a box that contained all that she needed, strung up her hammock, and made herself at home. She would live there for the next two years, quickly becoming part of the family.

In the early 1970s, many of the settlers had been given 100-hectare plots along the Transamazon Highway. The government had provided each family with the material to build a shack for themselves and with enough food supplies to last six months. If families had some education, were generally in good health, and willing to go, the government had even flown them into the area from many parts of Brazil. By the time Dorothy reached these remote settlements, however, the government incentives had disappeared. Now most of the people came on their own with very few belongings, and they were not given any help to get started.

Dorothy managed to visit the families and encouraged them to come together to form base communities. She had previously experienced how difficult it was to get the people of the north to trust the people of the south. In fact, some of the people were afraid of *her* initially because she *looked* like the people of the south who had driven many of them off their property. The southerners were descendants of the Italians and Germans who had flocked to Brazil after World War I. The northerners were of Indian-African-Portuguese descent. Gradually, however, the people began to form communities and to discuss how they could help each other. In doing so, trust began to grow.

When remembering those early days in Pará, Dorothy described her work:

> What I would like to say is that our whole emphasis at that time was to help those small groups, isolated out there in the woods, to create strong communal ties, and once they were created, to build strong CEBs [base communities]. The people needed to understand that if we did not organize our area of the Transamazon Highway, we would never grow, because we had been marginalized from the beginning. There were only people from northeast Brazil on this side of the highway. There were no villages, there was no infrastructure—the government provided infrastructure only for the southerners who lived in Altamira, on the other side of the highway. It was important, then, for the people to identify themselves publicly as organized—that this was who we were, and we weren't as unorganized as they might think we were, that we were more than just cheap labor. So we worked on creating infrastructure—a school, a little

parish center, a soccer field, roads that went into the forest, providing some modern things like a motor to clean their rice and little stores for selling their products. That was the women's part, to run the stores, and the men did the other tasks, and everyone was working tremendously hard.

Every time we got together, every month on the first Saturday of the month, the subject was land, how much land we could occupy, just occupying it and extending more and more into the woods. We talked with INCRA [the National Institute for Agrarian Reform] and had this big meeting with them. INCRA promised us help with more side roads into the woods and the construction of six permanent schools along the main road. That was a big joy, a big victory.

It was a five-day walk in the hot sun to Altamira for supplies such as coffee, sugar, medicine, or even cooking utensils. Dorothy had a plan. Perhaps the people could raise enough money to go into town, buy supplies, and then bring them home and sell them to the members of the community at a low price. The people countered that they did not have the money to buy the supplies to begin with. So Dorothy asked each family if they had any chickens. They all said they did. Then she asked if each family would give one chicken to the project. She told them she would take the chickens to town, sell them, and buy a pig.

After they agreed, Dorothy went into town, came back with a pathetic-looking sow, and asked each family to take turns caring for the pig until they fattened her up. When she became a decent size, they bred her and then had ten piglets to sell to get enough money for their supplies.

There was always the need to find a way to take some of the settlers needing medical care into town. Dorothy would drive the women who were ready to give birth to Casa de

Irma Seraphina, a facility run by the Sisters of the Precious Blood, where pregnant women, some as young as twelve years old, would go to deliver their babies and learn how to care for them before returning to the settlement. The babies could not be taken home until they had been vaccinated. The Casa also had a section where the poor could stay while they were being treated by doctors in the town. Many people in Altamira contributed to the Casa, providing fuel and food for those who went there. It was a place of comfort and refuge for those who had so little. Dorothy was always grateful to the sisters who took in the poor and helped them to get medical attention.

One of the first things the members of the base communities asked for was a school. Knowing that no teachers from the town were likely to want to come out into the forest to teach, Dorothy had to encourage some young women or men in the settlement to take up the profession. Most of the people had only a primary school education. When Dorothy found people who were willing to teach and who had at least a sixth-grade education, she would instruct them in teaching methods, drawing on her own experience as a primary school teacher. Then she would go to the government offices in Altamira, tell them about the school, and inform them that, by law, the state had to pay the teachers a salary. It often took a long time for the teachers to receive their pay. Rosario, a good friend of Dorothy's, taught for six months before she received any payment. Once a school got started, every neighboring small community wanted one and community members were happy to help build one for their children.

Since 1976, Dorothy had been a member of the CPT (Bishops' Pastoral Land Commission) and had attended its annual meetings. In 1982, when she went to the pastoral assembly and retreat in Altamira, she met Brother Geronimo, a Christian Brother who did teacher training for the prelature. Since the place where Dorothy lived was so far from the town, she convinced Brother Geronimo to come to her area and help her with the teachers. The prelature had acquired land for a school that the community had named Nazare and that they had already started building. Brother Geronimo wrote:

> The distances were so great for the teachers from Anapu whom Dorothy so devotedly encouraged to enter this profession and continue their studies that in 1983, with the Centro Nazare not totally completed, we began to give courses on this east side of the Transa [Transamazon Highway]. With little to no financial help, I found myself literally building alongside Dorothy's nephew (a NASA engineer who worked on Star Wars projects in the U.S. and had come on his vacation to Dorothy's) slinging clay and raising thatch to cover the roof of the building being built with the help of laborers from all the communities. In 1983, we initiated a course with duration of 2400 hours for forty-one female and nine male teachers. The courses were always held during the January/February vacation and again in July... I would be present to supervise and coordinate the courses.

Brother Geronimo would stay for days at Nazare, and he and Dorothy would talk long into the night about the needs of the people and the hardships they endured. He commented, "Wherever there was need for human support of the poor and simple people, this courageous and self-abnegating woman was present. The Bible and breviary were her daily companions and there she sought strength."

Dorothy had invited her nephew, Richard Stang, to come to Brazil for his vacation. Once he was there, she put him to work. In addition to helping to build the center in Nazare, Richard accompanied Dorothy when they hitchhiked three thousand kilometers to attend the trial and show support for two French priests who had been arrested for subversion.

Eventually, the community at Nazare prepared a house for Dorothy. It was a very simple house made of wood and clay. She had a small room with a table and some stools for meetings, a tiny bedroom where she had a cot to sleep on and a board to hold the books she used for the school, a small kitchen where there was a propane stove, and the usual outside shower and outhouse. In addition, they built a house for the instructors who came to give courses for the new teachers. One of the first things Dorothy did was to plant trees and flowers around the buildings. Wherever Dorothy went, she would plant flowers and encourage all the women to do the same with their homes.

When new teachers went to study at Nazare, they each had to bring with them some food to share. Some of them needed clothes to wear, which Dorothy found for them. Others had to bring their children with them, as there was no one to care for them at home. It was always a struggle to provide everything that was needed. Dorothy had to ask for money to provide transportation and housing for the teachers and the supplies they needed. Her letters to the Mission Society, the parishes in Ohio, and her friends resulted in a stream of funds that helped to keep her ministry going.

She would invite other Sisters of Notre Dame to come visit her at Nazare, and when she moved into her house a number of them came and shared time with her. She loved talking to the other sisters and hearing from the community in Ohio. Often she would almost plead with her family and the sisters at home to write to her, telling them how much she loved getting news of what was happening and hearing how they were. She nearly always signed her letters with "hugs and kisses."

In the first few years in the Anapu area, Dorothy helped the farmers start the Pioneer Association, the forerunner of the Farmers' Union. It gave dignity to the group that gathered to discuss farming techniques and ways of preserving the forest. Soon it became clear that the farmers needed some sound advice about farming, as the soil on the east side of the Transamazon—mostly sand under a thin layer of dirt—was not particularly fertile. The traditional "slash and burn" technique of farming, which involved clearing the land and burning what was left before planting new crops, was gradually destroying the soil. Dorothy encouraged some of the young men to go on to agricultural schools to learn to be agricultural technicians. They began a yearly "Farmer's Day" celebration each year to which many people from the distant communities would come, bringing sacks of rice and beans to share with each other as they enjoyed each other's company.

Instruction on farming methods was provided and, in addition, Dorothy taught geography. The people did not know how large their country was, or which countries bordered theirs and shared the Amazon Region. Realizing how important it was that they know the laws of the land, Dorothy taught the farmers about their rights and what the law said regarding ownership of their plots of land.

At least ten years before Dorothy had come to Anapu, INCRA had allocated very large tracts of land to farmers in the south who had seen a chance of expanding their herds and making more money. However, some of those people never came up to the Amazon Region. The land was untouched. According to the law, if land was not used productively for a period of from five to eight years, then ownership would revert back to the state. Much of the land in the area of Anapu was unused, which meant it was free for anyone to use. Many families were homesteading on this vacant land. But when the wealthy "owners," the people who had initially been given these large tracts, heard that loggers were looking to buy land, they became aggressive in evicting the homesteaders. No doubt it was a complex situation, legally speaking, but Dorothy spoke up for the poor farmers.

Even the property of Centro Nazare was threatened. On March 6, 1990, Dorothy wrote to the St. Raphael's Church Mission Office:

> It will take too long to write the whole story of a terrible injustice against our community right now, but I will try to give a few hints.
>
> Our community has a small piece of land here on the Transamazon Road. We have been occupying it since 1977. We have tried over and over again to get an official land document but we have had to be content with a simple preliminary document until official measurements are done.
>
> Well, we discovered recently that the land commissioner gave our neighbor a document that includes our small community area. We have tried to get some official help to rectify this situation, but with each step things get worse. Our mayor who lives two days away, as our county seat is up the Xingu River, has come several times and is coming again tomorrow. They say there is nothing to be done once an official document has been issued. The mayor simply says that we were betrayed. First our neighbor said that he would leave us with a small piece of land but now he has changed his mind after a group of conservative landowners convinced him that our work is communistic and that some day, if he isn't careful, we will take his land. Yes, he is poor, but he likes being a friend of the rich who have the power.
>
> Well, I came back to our center after four days holding small meetings in our base communities. A neighbor told me that a man had come to make an official measurement of our little piece of land and handed

the document over to the State. Thus we are considered invaders and the diocese no longer is the owner.

After two weeks of running around to official offices trying to straighten out the title to their land, Dorothy received a check for $904.00 from the Mission Office. A group of leaders from the base communities took the check to the bishop with a plan to buy a piece of land two kilometers from Centro Nazare that a farmer "by chance" was selling. They put another person forward as the buyer and obtained legal title to the land. Dorothy wrote to the benefactors that the plan was to

> dismantle the center, the church, two dormitories, a refectory, the kitchen, and our home and rebuild on the new land. Ask God's blessing. We feel the move will give us more peace. No more worry, as the man selling has an official document. These are the small ways the government has of trying to discourage our work and not being so obvious . . . We just want you to know that for us you are Divine Providence in action. We all love you so much for sharing. You give us certainty that our loving Father looks over us with great love. However, the Bishop intervened and eventually the land was declared property of the prelacy.

In 1984, Dorothy returned to Ohio to visit her ailing mother. Edna was happy to see her daughter for what proved to be the last time. Dorothy's father was grateful that she had had a chance to say good-bye to her mother, and he too was comforted by her visit. The following year, when it became clear that Edna was dying, Dorothy made haste to return again, but she arrived too late, just after her mother's death on February 13, 1985, at the age of eighty-seven.

In September 1986, Dorothy's two sisters, Mary and Marguerite (whom she called Maggie), visited her in Nazare.

They flew to Altamira from Belém and stayed in the bishop's house before taking the bus to Nazare. It seemed to them that "everyone knew Dorothy." Mary and Marguerite had no idea that Dorothy was living in such primitive conditions and were amazed at all she was doing. Bible studies, catechism lessons, farmers' meetings, visiting remote settlements, taking clothes and food to those in need—these were only some of the things that kept Dorothy busy. Her sisters found it hard to keep up with her.

At one point during the visit, Dorothy suggested that they go to a restaurant for lunch. While they were eating, Dorothy told them that she recognized a group of ranchers sitting at another table. When the men stood to leave, one of them came over to Dorothy, shook his fist in her face, and said in a menacing voice, "I know who you are. One day we will get you." Her two sisters did not understand what he was saying and asked Dorothy to translate the exchange. After explaining, she added, "This happens to me a lot." When her sisters expressed worry and fear, Dorothy stayed very calm as if the whole thing were a matter of no importance.

Mary and Marguerite slept on cots that night in the teachers' building at Nazare. They had to get used to the racket made by the cat catching mice and cockroaches beneath them. Dorothy had warned them to look into their shoes before putting them on in the morning, as they might find a tarantula or a scorpion in them. In spite of these little trials, they both managed well, and Dorothy was thrilled that they had come to visit. It was a "unique" experience for both her sisters, and they left with a deep sense of pride in what Dorothy was doing.

It became evident to Dorothy that the women of the settlements needed to be given more attention and respect. Along with several of them she started the Women's Association, empowering the local women to work on their own to better themselves. They started by reaching out to other women, helping them with health care and nutrition and ways of dealing with abuse and alcoholism. They also organized resale "stores" to help people in need. When, after a visit to the United States or one of the larger cities in Brazil, Dorothy received donations of clothing or household goods, she would give them to the women, who would sell them at a very low price. The stores began to make money for the settlers who then were able to sell cattle, pigs, and chickens as well as donated items to other settlers. Eventually, people even talked about starting a fruit cooperative and made plans for a building to process the fruit for market and make some money for their families.

With a large grant from St. Rafael's, one of the Ohio parishes, Dorothy planned to buy a small tractor to help the farmers get their produce out of the forest. The decision to buy the tractor was made by the base communities. But on August 2, 1993, after a year of negotiating to get the tractor, Dorothy wrote a long letter to the parish explaining why the tractor was still in the store. In her letter she expressed concern that the parishioners might have "lost confidence" in them because they had changed their minds. She wanted to explain what had happened and, in doing so, she detailed some of the problems she was facing:

> In August, 1992, we received your letter saying that you could reach the $10,000 [the original request]. I made a quick survey of prices and in six months the price was $14,000. We began then to negotiate seriously with a firm. We were counseled to not buy the $14,000 tractor, as the most it could pull up our steep hills was a ton. Going down the hill we needed more horsepower to keep the tractor from tipping. We then quickly searched for another $3,000 to buy a 50 horsepower tractor and not the 35 horsepower model that was $14,000. We paid for the tractor and it was ordered.

It was not shipped, however, until the following April, by which time the road had been washed out and it was impossible to even consider bringing the tractor to Anapu until June during the dry season. In the meantime, Brazil was experiencing runaway inflation. Dorothy explained:

> Our economy had gone rampant. What is manufactured by big firms as well as oil, etc., rises in price weekly Our produce—rice, beans and corn—cannot compete. We did surveys after many frantic meetings on what the price would be to bring a sack of rice or corn on the tractor to our main road. The price to ship the tractor was getting higher each week...We are on the brink of a military takeover again. We have not lost hope and struggle each day for clarity as to what to do...The decision made at our meeting on Saturday the 5th of June was to try to sell our tractor and buy a 3/4 truck, one that carries five to six tons ...The men say that they can make the road into the woods passable for this size truck. It costs less to run a truck than a tractor. A truck can carry more and is better for going up and down our difficult roads. The big issue is what is to be charged in freight to carry the produce.

In this letter one can sense her dilemma, knowing that the people who had sent the check for the tractor were wondering why the community had changed its mind and what had become of the money. Dorothy wanted to reassure the donors, but she also was working with a group of people who had no previous experience of doing anything like buying a truck and maintaining it. She anticipated the donors' questions when she wrote in the same letter,

> You might ask why we didn't calculate all this before. Good question! We are working with the poorest of

the poor who have never dealt with any mechanical object in their lives. I cannot make all the decisions. They are learning to be responsible. This takes time. One has an idea—another has another—and we are many. We try to listen to each and act on the knowledge we have. We hope . . . we are not losing your confidence, as we already know that those in the first world are better prepared in their thinking than we, but here the people have been enslaved financially and still are. We are so grateful for your help and we hope that with your help we can grow in our organizational programming. Yes, we still make errors in our calculating and planning. Bear with us.

At the end of the letter, Dorothy explained that the group had hoped a tractor would help bring their produce out of the forest to the main road where a truck could take it to town, but then they realized that doing all that would "eat up all the value of the products." She mentioned that she was looking forward to a visit from some St. Raphael parishioners and hoped that among them there would be someone who understood inflation "and a bit of primitive farming. We are trying to span generations of progress."

Finally, the community decided to purchase the truck, which went once a week into Altamira with their sacks of beans, rice, and corn. The group had to figure our how much to charge each farmer to transport his produce in order to pay for the gasoline and the upkeep of the truck. It was a learning experience for everyone.

Sister Dorothy ended her letter on a note of hope, saying that on August 7 they were going to begin the "Santa Missão Popular on the Transamazonia," a meeting of about one hundred missionaries, priests, sisters, and lay leaders from all over their region who were coming to "help us with our forty-four communities." It was to be held at their new St. Raphael Center in Anapu, which was just about finished. In addition, she said that they had received money to help build "our little laboratory for exams for worms, malaria, and leprosy." The mission was to end on August 15 and then she hoped to get back to the business of selling the tractor and buying the truck.

On one occasion, a group of settlers, encouraged by Dorothy, staged a protest against the local government that had received money to fix the Transamazon Highway in the area but had not done so. For three days, the settlers camped out on a bridge, blocking traffic. Finally, the government conceded and fixed the worst parts of the road. The farmers felt the power of their united efforts and became more confident in their abilities to bring about change.

Another piece of equipment that brought the people together and helped them was a rice husker. With a generator for electricity, again purchased through a grant given to Dorothy, the rice husker liberated the women from the task of having to husk the rice by hand. The farmers were able to cull much more of their rice without wasting it and, as a result, they could plant even more rice and have some to sell. The husker was put in a building that was large enough for storing sacks of rice and protecting them from the rain and from rodents, problems many of the families had to deal with in their own homes. The latter problem was solved when the center provided the farmers with cats, the best protection against rodents.

The base communities were growing in strength and confidence. The people saw Dorothy as their teacher, friend, and mentor. Dorothy knew about farming and shared with the farmers what she had learned from the classes she had taken in order to learn more about the land and its productivity. She wanted the people to have a cash crop so that they could earn enough to send their children to school and live with dignity. Often she would say to them, "You want to provide for your children and watch them grow. We are children of God. Don't you think that God wishes to provide for us as well?"

Whenever she heard of a family who had been expelled from their land by the land sharks, Dorothy would try to find some money to help them to buy a plot of land for themselves. Often members of the base communities would offer to help support the family as well. The people were learning to care for one another and share with each other. They were becoming a Christian community and learning what it means to put the lessons of scripture into practice.

7

HUNGER FOR JUSTICE

In November 1987, Dorothy wrote, "Our situation here in Brazil is worse each day as the wealthy make their plans to exterminate by hunger the needy. But God is good with His people." In fact, it was reported that millions of Brazilians in northeast Brazil were living a lifestyle comparable to that in the poorest parts of Africa, and that they were stunted in body and brain development due to malnutrition. "Their life expectancy is lower than it is in southern Brazil."

Hunger drove thousands of people to the cities hoping to find work, but once they got there, they found they could hardly keep pace with the rate of inflation—which was as high as 250 percent in 1983, while wages had increased by only 90 percent. Beggars lined the streets and there were instances of people fighting over garbage.

In 1985, after more than twenty years of rule, the military had peacefully retreated from power, yielding to the election of a civilian president, Tancredo Neves. On the eve of his inauguration, the elected president took ill. He died before assuming office and the vice president, José Sarney, an ally of the wealthy, became president. The new government attempted to decentralize power by giving the states more autonomy.

However, because Brazil is a very large country, it was extremely difficult to monitor how effectively the states were implementing federal policies. In addition to problems caused by inferior transportation and communication, the states were divided into municipalities comprised of a central urban setting and several surrounding urban or rural areas. "Finding a middle ground between the extremes of oppressive centralized authoritarianism and total state autonomy continues to be an obstacle to efficient and effective governance in Brazil," Dorothy wrote. "The federal government remains dependent on the willing cooperation of state and local authorities to carry out its decisions. With their broad responsibilities and powers, however, state and municipal governments often pick and choose which federal policies they will enforce and which they will ignore." As a result, *de facto* authority in remote areas, like the region around Anapu, rested in the hands of an oligarchy of wealthy landowners, people with their own security forces, able to pay for the cooperation of the police, who, in most cases, were not in a position to turn down their offers.

Dorothy sent a report to Ohio entitled "Decolonization Alert," which stated:

> Things here have reached a peak of human suffering I have never before experienced. The streets are filled with people begging, people who have never before done so in their lives. The government has created a type of emergency work that is nothing short of slave labor…the politicians enlist only the people who support them politically.

At the Bishops' Synod in 1983, Bishop Aloisio Lorscheider said that "Christians cannot remain indifferent before an unjust society because this is collaborating with sin; that First World Churches must help in the Third World not only with material aid but above all by the denunciation of injustice." Members of the hierarchy who heeded his message paid the price of siding with the poor. In 1987, Dorothy wrote to the sisters:

> Our Bishop D. Erwin with two young priests and a young teenage girl much involved in community work were going to this camp-in on Friday the 15th

to celebrate Mass at 2:00 in the afternoon. This site is 45 kilometers from Altamira. They had gone some 23 kilometers and were going up a steep incline with another car in front of them. A truck was coming down. All of a sudden our Bishop saw the truck aim for him. The next we knew there was a man here in Altamira, asking for the priest's house. I offered to help when he told me his reason. He had just brought our Bishop, one of the priests, and the young girl to the hospital. He had left the other priest, as he was dead. We ran for help. The steering wheel saved our Bishop, but his chest, back, mouth, and nose are much offended. We do not know too much as yet, since they were flown to Belém. The young priest who died was Father Tore from Sardinia, Italy. They are making plans to fly him back as he is an only son...Our Bishop is much threatened these days and this is just one of the attempts. You can imagine our town of Altamira... One poor old lady cried out in her agony, looking up to heaven, "It was not you, my Father, that took Father Tore from us but the hate and evil of the rich that planned his death. These rich hold such huge land areas and thus we die daily of hunger." Her cry was a terrible cry calling forth vengeance that only God can bring. Heavy hearts...

Dorothy, too, had received warnings and threats from the ranchers and land thieves in the area. She had escaped one attempt on her life when she and twenty-seven farm workers hid in a dump truck with high walls as the land sharks searched for them. Anapu had drawn simple farmers seeking opportunities, but it had also drawn fugitives and adventurers from Marabá, Tocantins, and Maranhão who plundered and murdered along the Transamazon Highway.

In Nazare, Dorothy kept teaching the members of the base communities about their rights. She was always seen with her plastic shoulder bag containing maps, a copy of the Brazilian constitution, and her well-worn Bible. Because of the land sharks and because even the poor farmers were often confused about just what land belonged to them, Dorothy frequently went to INCRA asking for legal documents that established the right of ownership for people who were threatened with eviction. Disputes were often brought before local judges to decide.

One such case ended happily for a poor farmer. Joanna and her family squatted on land outside of Anapu, which they considered free after the former owner had done nothing with it for over ten years. One day, a rancher whose large tract of land was next to theirs appeared while Joanna was alone. He had her house surrounded by gunmen. She insisted that the land was hers. Fortunately, the rancher and the gunmen retreated. But soon the rancher started to build a fence around their property, cutting them off from the community. By night, Joanna's husband and brother filled in the holes meant for the fence posts, but the rancher complained to the police that the farmer was harassing him. Finally the rancher agreed with the farmer to take the matter before a judge. After hearing both sides of the case, the judge settled in the farmer's favor. INCRA representatives came as well and confirmed that the farmer had made the land productive, thus confirming Joanna and her family's ownership of the land. In such cases, the outcome depended totally on the integrity of the judge; some judges simply took bribes from the ranchers and decided against the farmers. In this case, Joanna was courageous enough to defend her rights. Not all were prepared to stand their ground. Often, at the first sign of men brandishing guns, the farmers would surrender without a fight. There had been enough killings to justify their fear.

To help the farmers stay on their land, Dorothy was always trying to find money to lend them so they could buy their property. They would pay her back with rice or beans or whatever vegetables they could grow. Most of the farmers never had worked with money before. Some were used to trading in vouchers provided by the landowners who employed them. Others had always relied on barter. Dorothy had to teach them the intricacies of using money, opening a bank account, or even knowing what to do in a bank. Some of the banks in Altamira helped the farmers and treated them fairly. Dorothy knew which banks she could trust.

Gradually, as the teacher training classes progressed, some of the schools were able to teach the children up to the fifth grade level. The government did pay teachers and in some cases, helped to build schools or improve them. In fact, the school at Nazare was able to lay cement floors. Dorothy and the teachers tried to encourage students to go to Altamira to continue their schooling at least up to the eighth grade, but that meant that the students had to find people who would take them into their homes while they were attending school. Those who had relatives in town were the lucky ones. Once they finished the eighth grade, Dorothy would try to convince them to return to the area and teach in the schools near their homes. She did not always succeed in convincing the young people to return to their shacks in the forest after they had seen opportunities in the city.

Wherever she went, Dorothy made a special effort to reach out to the teenagers, as she saw in them the future of the community. She had meetings with the young girls at Centro Nazare, encouraging them to continue their studies, teaching them the Bible, conducting missions for them during which she taught them how to pray, and preparing them for the sacrament of confirmation. Eventually, she invited one or two of them to live with her at Nazare and join the pastoral team. They became catechists and helped out with the youth groups. She also taught them how to plant trees, flowers, and vegetables around the center. She would encourage them to "show their beautiful smiles" to those they met. She herself was recognized as the person with the beautiful smile. Nearly every picture that was taken of Dorothy during her lifetime shows her smiling as she taught, visited, or listened to the people.

Sister Eliska Durovic came to spend some time with Dorothy and entered into the ministry with her. Eliska also saw some of the young women as potential Sisters of Notre Dame. She and Dorothy spoke to some of them about the congregation and encouraged them to think about the possibility of joining the community as members.

Sister Jo Anne Depweg, Dorothy's friend from Coroatá, also came for a while and she, too, talked about encouraging new members to carry on the work of the sisters in Brazil. At the beginning of 1990, Dorothy and Jo Anne sent a proposal to the Archdiocesan Mission Office in Cincinnati requesting a $30,000 grant for a formation program to prepare young Brazilian women to take on leadership positions in a church struggling to address issues of social justice. The financial assistance would support five women for five years as they worked with and became Sisters of Notre Dame ministering to the most oppressed groups in both the rural and urban areas of Brazil. The program was to include personal development as well as formal study, always with an emphasis on the desire to work with the poor. By October of that same year, the sisters were thrilled when they received a letter telling them that their proposal had been accepted and that they would be receiving $10,000 a year for three years from the Mission Office. Dorothy saw that as another sign of God's blessings on their work.

Dorothy had her eye on Maria and Sandra, two young women she had known since they were children. She was sure that they might be Sisters of Notre Dame one day. Dorothy and Sister Eliska met Maria Sousa Arruda when she was only eight years old. Her family lived in a remote area in the Anapu region and when they saw two white women approaching them they thought that the women were Americans coming to tell them that they owned their land. Dorothy had quickly dispelled their fears and explained that they were there to form a community. Maria's father gathered some of the people from three nearby houses and together they said the rosary. That was the beginning of a long and close relationship between Dorothy and Maria's family. Maria's father became a leader in the base community that began to be formed at the time of Dorothy's visit. Two years later a school was established. Maria began school when she was nine years old, and after completing third grade she went to Altamira to live with her aunt until she had finished the eighth grade. At this point she was seventeen years old, and Dorothy asked her if she would consider coming back and teaching at the school in her community, since the teacher there had moved away. Maria agreed to do this and during the next two years she came to know Dorothy better. She was deeply touched by Dorothy's joy and hope for the people, and when she was asked to move to Nazare to live with the little community that was forming there, she went willingly. She felt a part of the pastoral team, especially when Dorothy said to her, "From here on I will consider you one of us." Maria taught catechism and helped with the youth groups and the meetings of the Women's Association. Thanks to Dorothy, Maria began to overcome her fears and to feel that there was a possibility opening up to do something for her people, to make a difference in their lives.

Sandra Araujo Dos Santos had also known Dorothy for years, having met her at the age of eleven when her parents were invited to join the Pioneer Association. Within a year after having joined, using money from the revolving fund of that group, they were able to purchase their land. When she was twelve, Sandra began attending literacy classes conducted by Brother Nestor from Altamira and Dorothy. Sandra's parents saw Dorothy as a woman totally dedicated to the people, "a different type of religious who lived alone and helped the people think for themselves." Sandra, however, saw her then as "a dreamer, a radical, and a very stubborn woman." Shortly afterwards, Sandra moved into the town of Anapu and lived with close friends of Dorothy in order to continue her studies through the eighth grade. As she saw more of Dorothy, she grew very fond of her.

After completing elementary school, Sandra returned to her home and began to teach in the school there. She also participated in the missions at Centro Nazare, prepared for confirmation, and went to the "Encounters for Vocations" with Sister Jo Anne at St. Raphael's, the meeting place Dorothy had built in Anapu. She had a boyfriend at the time, but remembers Sister Jo Anne saying to her, "You are not a sister yet, but I think God is calling you." She was given a book about St. Julie. Afterwards she returned home from the encounter saying to herself, "I think this saint really existed." She did not know what it was to be a sister, but there was definitely "something there."

By 1995, at the age of eighteen, Sandra had moved to Centro Nazare to be part of the small live-in community there. She did not yet know Maria, but she had already met Sister Katy Webster, another Sister of Notre Dame. When asked "Why have you come to live with us?" Sandra replied, "Because I was invited. I have come here because I want to be some kind of prophet. I want to work in the communities because I think this is great work." Later, when asked what it was like at Nazare, she described the community rhythm as "Wednesday 'til Sunday in the [base] communities; Monday wash clothes; Tuesday is community day." She, too, became a member of the pastoral team. She and Maria met each week with their mentors, Katy and Dorothy, to evaluate what was happening and reflect on their mission.

At the end of the first year, Dorothy and Katy asked Maria and Sandra if they would consider themselves candidates for religious life. They were invited to spend a second year considering their options. Dorothy even said, "If you are not going to be a religious, we will have to leave the openings for others," which Sandra found rather humorous because she "didn't see anyone knocking down the door." But it was during this time that Sandra felt a genuine call to a religious vocation. She said, "I was told to think about it, so I began to think. I talked to St. Julie: 'Well, I am here and I do not know what I want, but you are in charge of this thing, so you have to speak to me.' When I fell asleep, Julie appeared to me, smiling, and said, 'Stay with us.'" Sandra knew then that God was drawing her toward a religious vocation. Maria, too, reflected on the challenge of a long-term commitment and found it "scary" but, in the end, she felt she needed the challenge and together both young women said, "Let's go for it."

Maria and Sandra became more involved with the larger group of Sisters of Notre Dame in Brazil. They participated in the spirituality days with the sisters and then in a retreat in Belém to discern their vocations. At the end of 1998, they wrote their letters of intent to request entrance into the congregation. The sisters, who had gathered from the various missions in Brazil at their annual assembly, gave an enthusiastic "yes" to their reception into the community. Then the two packed their bags and moved into a house in Altamira that the sisters had rented. Sister Jane Dwyer and Sister Katy Webster moved in with them to establish a formation community. Dorothy arranged for both young women to go to the Catholic high school in Altamira, which was conducted by the Precious Blood Sisters, who gave them full scholarships.

In reflecting on their experience of Dorothy, Sandra remembers that Dorothy came often to Altamira, or she and Maria would visit Dorothy in Centro Nazare, and that she always encouraged them to do well in their studies. Sandra says,

> I just know that Dorothy had a lot of faith. She was certain that God would be with the people in their struggle. I remember she loved the psalms and the Magnificat. For me, Dorothy's spirituality was always cosmic. Everything revealed God's presence to her. She had a great capacity to forgive because there were people included in the community who had betrayed her and she would receive them in her home. She saw potential in everyone. She taught much more by the way she lived than by words. I always felt she put a lot of trust in me.

Perhaps Dorothy had shared something of the spirit she expressed when she celebrated her birthday in 1991. In a letter dated November 11, 1991, she wrote to her family and friends:

> Well, I'm celebrating my 60 years young and 25 of them in Brazil. Just want to shout to the world that they've been good and you've in some way helped to make them so meaningful to me...including my great family I married into at 17, Notre Dame. That I've been able to live, love, be loved and work with the Brazilian people, help them find confidence in themselves, to profoundly sense God's presence in their lives and then be a creative influence in society from which a more human society can be born, I thank all of you. It's a chain reaction. We can give positive input-energy into life but we need to be charged also.
>
> ...In the midst of all this violence there are many small communities that have learned the secret of life...sharing, solidarity, confidence, equality, pardon, working together. It doesn't matter what the religious beliefs are as long as human values guide them. God is present...generator and sustainer of all life. Thus life is productive and transforming in the midst of all this.

Dorothy was changing, too. Sustained by her faith, her prayer life, and other Sisters of Notre Dame, she was growing in a holiness rooted in a passion for God, justice, and a love for her poor. Over the years St. Julie has inspired thousands of women to give of themselves generously to service out of love. Dorothy was living that dream in the forests of the Amazon. And, as with Christ and Julie before her, it was impossible for Dorothy to do so without paying the cost.

8

LOVE OF CREATION

In 1972, a United Nations conference on the human environment held in Stockholm resulted in the establishment
of a United Nations Environment Program to act as a global
catalyst for action to protect the earth's environment. However, little was done by any nation to integrate environmental
concerns into economic planning and decision-making. As a
result, the process of environmental degradation continued
unimpeded. And one of the most devastating aspects of the
deterioration of the world's natural resources was the destruction of the Amazon rain forest.

By the 1990s, the whole world was becoming aware of
the impact of deforestation of the Amazon and its effects on
biodiversity, hydrology, and climate. A little-known fact is
that 25 percent of all pharmaceutical products used in the
world come from Amazon plant species. Much of the development of the Amazon region—particularly logging, ranching, and mining, as well as the construction of roads and
dams—was contributing to the environmental destruction of
the area. Such destruction has had an enormous effect on
global environmental and ecological health as well as on the
economic future of Brazil.

Dorothy knew what was happening to the forests in her
region. She had seen what happened when loggers left thousands of acres of land barren. According to a U.N. report,
"The region of Pará, where much of the conflict over land in
the Amazon occurs, has lost 70 percent of its vegetation to

various predatory forms of development and represents one-third of the total Amazon deforestation in Brazil. Figures on yearly rates of deforestation range from 17,000 square kilometers to 30,000 square kilometers, with recent satellite images suggesting that deforestation is occurring at twice the rate previously thought." No wonder Dorothy frequently wore a tee shirt with the words, "*A morte da floresta e o fim da nossa vida*" (the death of the forest is the end of our lives). As she saw the beauty of the forest being ravaged, she became more passionate about saving it from destruction. With all she saw happening around her, it is not surprising that Dorothy was attracted to a program called the "Institute of Culture and Creation Spirituality" at Holy Names College in California. In December 1991 that is where she went on sabbatical leave from her work in Brazil. It proved to be just what she needed at the time.

Creation Spirituality was not entirely a new idea. From the time of the Middle Ages, Christian mystical theologians such as Hildegarde of Bingen, Francis of Assisi, Mechtild of Magdeburg, Meister Eckhart, Julian of Norwich, and Nicolas of Cusa had been extolling the grandeur and beauty of God as seen in all of creation. In more modern times, Pierre Teilhard de Chardin, S.J., a scientist and Jesuit priest who died in 1955, had written extensively about the "Divine Milieu," extolling the presence of God in the evolving mystery of the cosmos.

More recently, Matthew Fox, director of the program at Holy Names College, had written a book entitled *Original Blessing*, which he juxtaposed to the more traditional doctrine of "original sin." While he admitted that our good "original self" can be obscured and distorted by alienation and sin, he proposed an emphasis on the discovery of our authentic nature as part of the creation that God termed "very good." Fox argued the need to reconnect the relationship between reason and intuition, consciousness and embodiment, human beings and other living creatures, both animals and plants. Embracing the good of all creation "unleashes vitality, creativity

and playfulness," he wrote. "It is generous, mutually affirm-
ing of diversity and non-competitive."

What was even more compelling for Dorothy was the
insight that Creation Spirituality was naturally allied with
liberation theology and the struggles for justice in Latin
America. In patriarchal societies there was a natural connec-
tion between the abuse of women, the exploitation of the
poor, and the abuse of nature. Dorothy had seen all of this
up close. One of her colleagues recalls that during their orientation session, Dorothy "cried and cried" when telling
the others that she had just arrived from Brazil and was in a
state of shock. "She had had no intermediary experience in
processing the stark differences between the first and fourth
worlds. She expressed her sadness at seeing the stark contrast between the excessive wealth here and the poverty
there." But, according to Marlene DeNardo, one of the instructors who had known Dorothy for years, she had a zest
for life in spite of her sorrows. She enjoyed all of life, eating, walking in the forest, swimming in the ocean, listening
to the stories of the people. With the warmth of her personality and her wonderful smile, she lived out the Gospel
story by following the way of Jesus. Her companions in the
program came to love her.

Fox talked about "ecojustice" as essential for planetary
survival and human ethics. He went further, to say that without ecojustice we are crucifying the Christ all over again in
the form of the destruction of forests, sources of water, di-
verse species, the very air we breathe, and the soil that sustains us. During Holy Week of 1992, Fox asked his students
to create a Holy Week ritual. Sharon Abercrombie, a classmate of Dorothy, recalls one particular ritual designed by a
student from Perth, Australia. He created a series of "ecological stations," which he fashioned after the Stations of the
Cross, placing these depictions of the destruction of the earth
across the campus. When the students gathered on the hill-

side in a grove of trees for the crucifixion station, the student nailed to a tree a picture of the earth taken from outer space. Sharon adds, "The thought that comes to me right now is that Dot knew all about the crucifixion of the earth via the rain forest...and how she was trying to resurrect it and the poor people there by teaching them sustainable farming methods." All of these themes resonated in Dorothy's heart, validating her passion for justice for people and nature.

Reclaiming suppressed creativity was another goal of Creation Spirituality. Dorothy reveled in her rediscovery of a talent for painting and ceramics. She painted large shamrocks on her dormitory door in preparation for St. Patrick's Day, then invited a group from her program to come to her room for a party. She rejoiced in music and dance, in which she saw a reflection of larger spiritual powers and life energies. After a lonely life in Brazil, her time in the program helped her to relish the presence of others who shared her love of life and for the earth. Describing the program to her friend, Sister Barbara English, she said, "It was a tremendous moment for me, a highlight. It really helped me deepen in relation to ecology, which I had embraced very much in my heart for years, even when I was in Arizona in the desert. Marlene DeNardo and Matthew Fox opened up another dimension of my faith through reflections on my Irish heritage...It was a tremendous lift!"

When she finished the semester, many of Dorothy's family and friends saw a change in her. Some described her as being "freer," more relaxed, and more in touch with herself. She became more comfortable with her emotions and seemed to have greater ease expressing them more readily. She began to talk about God as "Mother" or as "Father/ Mother" and to relate to the feminine side of God. She even made a ceramic feminine God figure, which she took back to Brazil and treasured. Family and friends detected the emergence of a more playful, passionate, creative Dorothy who had been hidden for a while under the weight of so many violent, sorrowful experiences. Although always remarkably resilient and optimistic about the goodness of people, Dorothy now rejoiced more than ever in that belief.

Shortly after returning to Brazil, Dorothy attended the historic Earth Summit in Rio de Janeiro, from June 3 to 14, 1992. This U.N. conference on environmental development drew over a hundred thousand people from all over the world. There were twenty-four hundred people representing non-governmental organizations (NGOs) attending a parallel NGO forum. It was the largest group that had ever gathered to discuss environmental issues. The goal of the Earth Summit was to formulate an understanding of development that would support socioeconomic development while preventing the continued deterioration of the environment. It was hoped that the Earth Summit could lay a foundation for a global partnership between the developing and the first-world nations based on mutual need and common interests that would ensure a healthy future for the planet.

"Agenda 21" was adopted by 108 heads of states. It included three major agreements: a comprehensive program of global action in all areas of sustainable development; the Rio Declaration on Environment and Development, a series of principles defining the rights and responsibilities of states; and the Statement of Forest Principles—a set of principles to guide the sustainable management of forests worldwide. Agenda 21 contained detailed proposals for action, including ways of preventing deforestation and promoting sustainable agriculture. But, for all the idealism unleashed in this conference in Brazil, the principles and proposals were rarely, if ever, carried out in the region of the Amazon.

Dorothy wrote to her family on July 24, 1992, "Really the world scene is not good. Tell all the family that we must make great efforts to save our planet. Mother Earth is not able to provide anymore. Her water and air are poisoned and her soil is dying of exaggerated use of chemicals, all in the name of profit...Pray for all of us and for a world where all can live—plants, animals, and humans in peace and harmony."

She returned to Nazare more determined than ever to help reclaim the forest. In a letter to her sister Barbara on November 1, 1992, she wrote: "We are a bit worried here, as it is terribly warm and no rain. All is drying, and so there are fast-fires in the forest. Can you imagine this?! Yes, ecology is the talk of the day. I've been going here and there to help talk about the need to replant our forest." She and her farmers started to plant cedar and mahogany trees as part of the restoration program. On October 1, 1993, she wrote: "Yes, we're reforesting with cedar, mahogany, and other noble trees from the forest. We hope to replant some 30,000 to 40,000 this year. In relation to the thousands cut down it is few, but then we must begin. Takes time to raise awareness."

Dorothy helped the rural farmers see that the "slash and burn" method of farming was depleting the nutritional value of the soil after two or three plantings. Those who had enough money to buy fertilizer only contributed to the problem by adding poisonous chemicals to the water. She encouraged the farmers to try using oxen to plow the fields instead of burning off the vegetation. On April 22, 1995, she wrote:

Earth Day...so much to celebrate...World news you have each day and it seems that human relations around the globe get worse. But for sure there is HOPE alive. Guess what! We have a group that is starting to farm with oxen. Instead of burning a piece of land to plant each year, they hope to turn over the soil and plow under what nutrients are there. We hope this will be one of many groups.

Remembering her days studying Creation Spirituality, Dorothy continued to bask in its values. "Matt Fox and all his co-writers and thinkers keep my heart aglow with new hope for humanity if we heed his counsel," she wrote in January 1994. In another letter she added, "I'm reading *Liberating Gifts for the People of the Earth* by Matt Fox. He is one that fills my mind and heart with new life in spite of so much that is violent in our world." Later she wrote that she was continuing to learn "how to help people recapture a relationship with 'Mother Earth' that is tender and kind—God's gift to us to live more fully as part of our cosmic universe." Her brother David says, "She truly believed that God was in all things. And she felt enormous pain when she'd see a mahogany tree burned to the ground—a thousand years of divine evolution destroyed in a day." She was to carry the tenets of Creation Spirituality with her for the rest of her days.

Dorothy was well aware of the dangers she faced in confronting the loggers and the ranchers. She knew the story of Chico Mendes who had been murdered because he believed in the same things she did. He was a simple rubber-tapper who had begun organizing the workers in nonviolent protests against those who were raping the forest and threatening their livelihood. He became a leader in the fight to save the forest and to advocate sustainable use of the land. Because of his work, the plight of the rubber-tappers began to receive international attention. In 1985, Mendes founded the National Council of Rubber Tappers and traveled to Washington, DC, at the invitation of the Environmental Defense and National Wildlife Federation, bringing the struggle of the workers and the threat to the Amazon into sharp focus for the international community. He convinced the Inter-American Bank to suspend its loan to the Brazilian government for building a road into the forest. The road, he argued, would be a disaster for the people of Acre unless it could be redesigned to protect the forest and its inhabitants. He proposed that certain areas of land be designated as reserves where rubber-tappers and other extractivists could live and work in ways that would preserve the forest. The reserves would be managed by members of the local communities. The bank agreed to his plan.

In 1988, a final confrontation cost Chico Mendes his life when he led the Xapuri Rural Workers Union in an effort to stop a cattle rancher, Darly Alves da Silva, from deforesting an area designated as a reserve. The union won the legal rights to the reserve. Mendes had also obtained a warrant for the arrest of Alves for murdering a man in another state. He took the warrant to the federal police in the municipality where Alves lived, but the police did nothing. Alves, in turn, publicly swore that he would kill Mendes. On December 22, 1988, Alves's son shot Mendes behind his house in Xapuri, Acre.

The story of the murder of Chico Mendes circled the globe and, for the first time in the history of land conflicts in Brazil, in the 1980s the murderers—Alves and his son—were arrested, convicted, and jailed. The reserve that Chico Mendes lived and died for is now known as the Chico Mendes Extractive Reserve and is one of twenty-one reserves covering more than eight million acres declared federal reserves over the last decade. Like Dorothy, Mendes believed in the worth of the individual citizen's actions, the rights of the workers, and the cause of social justice. After his death, thirty union, church, human rights, political, and environmental organizations banded together to form the Chico Mendes Committee to continue the work he had begun. Knowing the fate of Mendes, Dorothy was aware of what the cost could be for continuing the struggle for land for the poor and facing the ranchers and loggers, but the fact that he had succeeded in getting land for the tappers only encouraged her to do the same for her farmers in Anapu.

Dorothy had always believed that the government would honor the principles spelled out during the Earth Summit for the preservation of the forest. After all, she was familiar with the Rio Declaration on Environment and Development and was especially concerned about some of its conclusions:

That human beings are at the center of concerns for sustainable development. They are entitled to a healthy and productive life in harmony with nature.

That eradicating poverty and reducing disparities in worldwide standards of living are "indispensable" for sustainable development.

That full participation of women is essential for achieving sustainable development.

These were just like the principles that she had embraced in working with her people. She believed that she could convince INCRA and IBAMA (Brazilian Institute for Renewable Natural Resources and the Environment), the agencies most responsible for implementing these principles, that setting up designated reserves for the rural farmers would protect them from the exploitation and abuse they were suffering at the hands of rapacious loggers and ranchers. But the loggers continued to cut and the ranchers continued to burn, contributing to the destruction not only of the forest but also of the ozone layer around the planet.

Sister Claire Callahan was mission coordinator for Africa and Latin America for the Sisters of Notre Dame. At the end of 1989, she wrote a report of her trip to Brazil in which she described her flight from Belém to Altamira. She wrote:

In this, as in my other air journeys that were to follow, I was introduced to the alarming devastation of the tropical rain forests. As you know, the rainforests hold millions of species of flora and fauna that are all part of a fragile ecosystem where even the most minute organism is indispensable to the continuance of life. The loss of one species means extinction for countless others which tears an irreparable rent in the fabric of life. Many of the Indians are trying to continue to live in a traditional way, relying on forest plants and animals to supply them with many of their life-sustaining needs. You will have read of some un-scrupulous rubber tappers of the Brazilian Amazon who abuse the privilege of harvesting the forest's valuable products and of those, like Chico Mendes, who give their lives to save this majestic wonder of our world. So much of what we use today, furniture, clothing, food and even cars [is made of materials that originated] in tropical forests. This precious, complex rainforest is being depleted faster than it can regenerate and from the little I viewed, destroyed be-yond hope of renewal. Large-scale agribusiness, the enormous external debt, the greed of already-wealthy landowners [all] help to devastate and defoliate the forests for personal profit. After witnessing the rav-aged land from the air, my thoughts were profoundly somber as we landed. I felt helpless until I realized that our sisters are there, trying to make a difference.

And, there on the airfield apron was one of them. Dorothy Stang (OH), smiling her welcome.

In spite of the difficulties, Dorothy remained optimistic, especially as she saw the base communities growing. She was very excited about a "Holy Mission" meeting that was held at Centro Nazare in 1993. The meeting drew about 130 lay-people representing the base ecclesial communities and ap-proximately 30 missionaries—priests, religious, and laypeople —from all over the state of Pará. Dorothy said, "We all lived out the mission for eight days. It was a fantastic thing! It was a celebration of all our work as CEBs [base ecclesial commu-nities] all those years." She could see the growth of the lead-ers, and the number of schools that had started. When she first arrived there had been seven schools, and now there were twenty-three. The community had grown accustomed to praying together and sharing scripture with each other. They had a mission coordinator and occasionally a priest from Belém so they could celebrate the Eucharist together. She rejoiced in the community spirit.

Dorothy continued to have meetings each month with the community leaders to discuss problems, pray, and learn more about the Bible. Regrettably, her work was not always appreciated by some of the clergy. It could have been that they were concerned about her practice, in the absence of a priest (which was the usual situation), of anointing the sick and even hearing the confessions of the dying. She brought the solace of the church to those who had been deprived of the sacraments for most of their lives. They were so far from any parish. Sometimes Dorothy could get a priest to go with her into the interior, but most of the time she had to lead the community as best she could in a communal prayer service. Yet, of one instance she said:

> When the priest came, he celebrated Mass, baptized children and took care of the sacraments. So we didn't do any more preparing for Eucharistic ministers or of the people for Baptisms, because the priest didn't like anything we did. We concentrated on the land struggles, on organizing communities, not so much in the sacramental way but in the evangelical way. We had Bible courses every year.

She had to have felt the criticism after all her hard work, but she nourished herself with her own deep prayer life. Those who lived with Dorothy knew that every morning she found a private place to pray. She always carried her Bible and her breviary wherever she went. Every time she met with a group in the forest, she invited them to pray together. Her energy and her courage sprang from her deep faith and her obvious love of God and the people.

In the midst of her work, she received word that her father was gravely ill. Her last visit with him had been in 1993 on her return from Namur, Belgium, where she had attended her first international meeting of the Sisters of Notre Dame. Later, she described that visit as a "real treasure." Her sister Norma, who was caring for their father, told Dorothy that he had a strong will and was fighting to live, despite a series of small strokes. In a letter to her family in November 1993 Dorothy described a phone conversation with her father:

> He told me that he loves me and that I should take care of myself. In my last conversation a month ago, he told me that he thanks God for Norma, that she gives him such a cozy life. I asked him if he talks and prays to Mom. He said she is in the next room. When I asked him if he talks to her each day, he said that she was right there in the room with him.

Then Dorothy wrote a prayer that expressed the anguish that was in her heart at that moment. She began:

> All that I can say my God is what does this macho church want of us women? We have given our all. [I have] even sacrificed my home, country, family, trust, to work among your people. God, my lover and Creator, I love You but I don't understand why they seek to destroy our simple life-joy-caring among the people. I never came to create hate or division but to build love, confidence, and caring among a beautiful, abandoned people. Does this have to be a part of life's struggle?
>
> Dear God, I come from a strong family. My Mom is a beautiful woman. She raised us all with a deep love and gave us strength to live as good loving people. Dad and Mom taught us to be responsible. Why then, O my loving Creator, do we have these human differences?
>
> Please, God, help me to be a presence of love-union-confidence-caring, desire that your people—

my people—be the best possible, that all that is strong and beautiful be reflected in their lives.

God, my Lover—you that wooed my heart to follow You even to other lands to serve—don't abandon me. I trust that You are with me—strengthen me daily—I'm fragile. I need You.

It was a difficult time and her heart ached at the thought of losing her beloved father. He did not easily express his emotions, even signing his letters to her "Your Father." But she knew they had a special bond. She received word of his impending death on May 2, 1994. She told Sister Barbara English:

I was on the Transamazon Highway when I got the message that my father was dying. There was nothing moving on the highway until about 9 PM that evening, when a motorcycle came along through lots of mud. Katy helped me and I got a ride with the motorcyclist. I strapped my backpack onto the back of the motorcycle and we started out on the trip. I talked the whole time to my Dad. He was still alive at that time, but he was in bad condition. I never got to see him alive again because he died on the next day, on my Mom's birthday. That was tough.

Dorothy made it back in Ohio in time for his funeral Mass on May 7 in St. Rita's Church in Dayton. There were so many memories in that church: her parents working in the Fall Festivals, singing in the choir, going to daily Mass together, being surrounded by the love of her family. She was anxious, as always, to get back to the people who needed her. After her father's death, Dayton would never be the same.

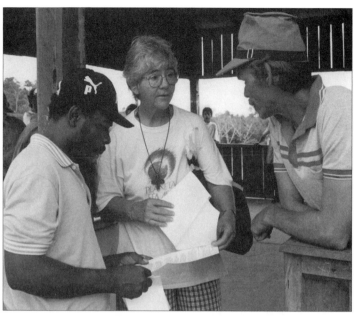

Dorothy working with farmers on deeds and sustainable farming projects.

Dorothy's bedroom in the sisters' house in Anapu.

Community Center in Boa Esperança.

The site of Dorothy's death.

Following an autopsy, Dorothy's body
was placed in a sealed casket.

Dorothy's funeral procession.

Dorothy's family at her grave.

9

BLESSED ARE THE PERSECUTED

The remote town of Anapu was situated at the end of one county and the beginning of another. Falling in between the two counties, it was overlooked by both of them. To get anything of benefit—whether building roads or settling land disputes—done for their community, the farmers had to travel to Belém or just do it themselves. Dorothy recognized the advantages for Anapu of becoming its own county, so she encouraged a group of settlers to go to Belém to get information from the agency in charge of the steps necessary to become a municipality. After that visit, they organized a huge campaign to collect signatures in favor of the idea. Not only would the rural farmers have a greater chance of getting their land disputes settled in their own county, but the Pioneer Association would be able to become a *bona fide* union as well.

The settlers worked a whole year preparing for the necessary election and setting up voting stations. Dorothy reported: "We provided transportation and food, because there was no outside help from the government and we had to do it ourselves. And we did it. On December 3, 1995, we had this magnificent election and it was almost entirely in favor of municipal status. On December 27 of that same year, the governor signed the official document declaring us a county. That was a tremendous thing for us!"

The next year, Dorothy and her team worked to prepare candidates for the municipal elections. Another group wanted to unite with them and proposed that its candidate run for mayor, with Dorothy's candidate running for vice-mayor. Unfortunately, her team decided against the proposal. That left room for a "dark horse" candidate with a lot of government money behind him. The two groups were divided and the "dark horse" won. Dorothy admitted, "It was a lesson! And it alerted us to the fact that there was a growing opposition to all this community work that we had been doing and that we had better be careful." In fact, as she explained,

> up to this point we had only recognized the opposition of a couple of strong landowners, like the one who bombed us out in 1984, Paulo Mendes, who shot up our people and a few others. But they acted in isolation from each other. They had nothing to do with each other. They were here and there, on their big ranches. So we weren't worried about them, but at this moment we began to see that they were starting to consolidate. The newly elected mayor allied himself with them and made a concerted effort to destroy us. They remain up until today a strong opposition.

Dorothy's community did get two councilmen elected and kept them working hard, but, she said, "we saw the handwriting on the wall, that we had to dig in harder because the opposition now was organized and more visible and that put us in a position of greater need."

In 1996, Dorothy heard news that a group of medical personnel from Arizona was going to Altamira to perform surgery for poor people. She decided that she would go into town and thank them for coming. Michael Sepulveda was on the team and describes what happened.

> The day we arrived, there were hundreds of people waiting at the clinic to be seen and hopefully selected to have their needs addressed. We saw people with

everything from skin lesions to bad burn scars, and many children with gross facial deformities, such as cleft palates and harelips, all of which needed to be surgically repaired. As it happens often times with these types of endeavors, things don't always go as planned. The English-speaking Brazilian nurse that we were promised had to cancel her trip to Altamira at the last minute. At the time, none of us on the team spoke much Portuguese. As you can imagine, it was going to be quite difficult to conduct a surgical mission for two weeks without being able to communicate in the same language as the patients and hospital staff we'd be working with. But, we were there and had to try to do the best we could.

The first day of surgeries went as we expected, very slow and inefficient, based in large part on our inability to communicate effectively with the hospital staff and patients. We all agreed it was going to be a long two weeks.

At the end of that first day, that evening, we were relaxing at the hotel [where we were staying]. There was a call from the lobby that someone was there to see us. It was Sister Dorothy. She introduced herself and told us the story of how she'd heard on the news that an American medical team from Arizona would be working in Altamira. She had made the day-and-a-half trip to Altamira from Anapu where she lived, all by herself in a little, beat-up, old Volkswagen through the jungle on dirt and muddy roads. She arrived [in] town that morning and went directly to the hospital where we were working. When she asked to see us, she was basically told by some of the hospital staff to leave . . . that we didn't have time to see her and we couldn't be bothered. So she left the hospital.

Well, after such a long trip, Sister Dorothy wasn't going to be denied. She made some inquiries, found out where we were staying and just showed up at the hotel. She told us her story of being an American Catholic missionary nun living in Brazil for the last twenty some odd years. She spoke of the many years she spent teaching as a young nun in Phoenix, Arizona, at a Catholic school named Most Holy Trinity. She was proud of her work in Arizona and quite obviously very fond of the many people she knew there. She was quite excited to know that we were also from Arizona and had felt compelled to make the long trip to Altamira, just to say hello and thank us for the work we were doing.

Well, that was it! With her charming and friendly personality, that ever-present smile, the soft voice and those piercing blue eyes, we all fell in love with her. Standing there before us was a true God-send! We told her about our problems at the hospital with communication. We immediately asked her, or maybe pleaded with her is more accurate, to please consider helping us with our work at the hospital for as long as she was able. She enthusiastically said yes, she was happy to help us as long as we needed her.

When we arrived at the hospital that next morning with Sister Dorothy, she walked right past those bewildered hospital staff that had kicked her out of the hospital the day before, as if nothing had happened. [She was] smiling and greeting them as she walked by.

With the addition of Sister Dorothy to our team, we were complete. We could now communicate through her, very effectively, exactly what we needed to our patients and the hospital staff. Everything began to run smoothly and efficiently. Of course, Sr. Dorothy wasn't just an interpreter. She expanded her role on the team. Constantly on the move, reassuring patients and their families by praying with them, joking with them and just putting them at ease. She was continuously cheering on our surgical team and the hospital staff with kind words of encouragement. Just being Sister Dorothy, spreading her joy and making everyone feel good.

This is only one small story in a lifetime full of many stories of compassion, courage, faith and absolute commitment to helping those in need and to the preservation of our precious environment.

Dorothy felt that moving into the small, dusty frontier town of Anapu would make it easier to reach the base ecclesial communities and to get more support from the town council. It was a town that was remarkable mostly for its muddy roads during the rainy season and its clouds of dust during the dry season. She built a small, simple house on the grounds belonging to the prelacy of Xingu. She planted trees and flowers around her house, and when she moved into it in 1998, it soon became a refuge for the poor and the frightened. Fr. Amaro, a young priest who had been mentored as a seminarian by Dorothy and was newly ordained, was assigned to what would become St. Lucy's Parish that same year, and he quickly became one of Dorothy's strongest supporters. He, too, sympathized with the hundreds of poor families moving into the area simply to find a place to live; many had been driven out of other areas by the landowners. The parish grew very quickly and Dorothy helped design some of the furnishings for the altar as well as statues to be carved by local artists.

During the summer of 1998, Dorothy returned to Ohio for rest and to prepare to celebrate at the Province Center in Reading, Ohio, her fifty years of religious life. It was a time of reconnecting with friends with whom she had entered the community and for visiting other friends and family. For four months, Dorothy enjoyed being with loved ones and having more time for prayer and reflection.

During this period, the Sisters of Notre Dame held a general chapter in England at which sisters representing all of the mission territories were present. Reports of the proceedings at the chapter came frequently. One of the actions the sisters at the meeting were asked to do was to write a letter to themselves that they thought the two foundresses, Julie Billiart and Françoise Blin de Bourdon, would have written to them. Dorothy heard of the request, and when she returned to Brazil, she did just the opposite: she wrote a letter to the two foundresses.

In her letter, she reveals the anguish she was experiencing at the time. Even while she was still in Ohio, she had shared with her best friend, Joan Krimm, that the "romance was over" in Brazil and that she was finding it difficult to go back. And yet she knew she needed to be there. She wrote:

My Dear Julie and Françoise,

I arrived back in Brazil very happy to have celebrated a wonderful life, unconcerned, enjoying good health, praising God every day with my friends. I thought that I would be ready to face whatever was ahead. You know something? I was wrong. I discovered that I was not at my best psychologically. I need time to live with the harsh reality that I have been away from for four months.

I feel shaken, my tranquility is being transformed, and my head is spinning. The reality is larger than I! Julie and Françoise, I so need to talk with you. I am convinced that you both know me. What is my reaction trying to say to me? Why am I not strong enough? I no longer know what to do.

Clearly, I see the effects of these times when new liberalism reigns and 80% of the people are discarded victims. For many years, I have taken on the cause of the people with my SND companions. During these years I have marveled at the captivating simplicity of the people—their way of speaking with God, their sharing of the best that they have. Together we faced many battles against the effects of feudalism that still dominates the poor.

During these years of walking with so many companions so dedicated to the struggle together with the oppressed people, I learned the value of solidarity. How I felt happy—fulfilled—nothing was too much!

Something is happening. The people who took on the struggle with the new evangelization of Basic Christian Communities are in the third age. I am trying to assess their lives, our movements, our church that opened their eyes to the Gospel that encouraged their hearts to struggle, like you, Julie, who spoke to the people in the fields in your time.

And now the system of government has grown, Françoise. I have learned how it has infiltrated the people, dividing them. I have never seen such fights among the leadership. The people know how to appraise different paths, create projects and move forward. But the help that comes from the government comes with a different orientation. It is that the individual works directly with the government and no longer in relationship with the co-operatives, associations, movements. Our leadership is forced by the government to direct according to the objectives of the government. Françoise, you understood the financial system of your times. Today it is more masked, delicate so as not to be perceived. The projects of the government are so weighted down by bureaucracy and take up so much of the time of the militant leaders that they lose contact with their base. The people are becoming poorer and are fighting among themselves.

And we, Notre Dame, find that we need, more than ever, solidarity, companionship, community among us so as not to lose the vision that we have had for our people since the beginning, the people of the reign of God here on earth. Our mission to be at the side of the people makes it urgent, as never before, to live the challenges of the Gospel and together enter into the third millennium with plans for an alternative society that gives LIFE.

Julie and Françoise, your life witness inspires us even today. May many courageous people join us. I ask that God deepen my faith so that I not lose my enthusiasm for the struggle of the people. That I can direct my companions who count on me.

Good night, Julie and Françoise, it is late and I want to send my warmest greetings to you. I await your response to bring me the strength of your support.

She signed her letter with "A kiss full of love, Dorothy, SND." The letter was found after her death; no one in Brazil guessed what agony she was enduring while facing the dangers that lay ahead of her.

At the Conference on Popular Health Methods held at St. Lucy's Parish Hall in March 2000, Dorothy wrote: "Well my greatest joy is seeing so many from all over our vast country—people from all our little communities in the woods—here at our center." She relished seeing the fruit of the labor of the pastoral teams as, she said, her "energies lessened." She acknowledged that "our modern world is full of wonderful inventions" that are expensive and that the wealthy enjoy. But, she added, "those who hold political power want all the latest so the rest of our population looks on from a distance."

Always hopeful, she continued in her letter to a donor:

But if we keep working, helping our people grow in education, their ability to speak up—organize—create within themselves a *spirit* guided by *The Spirit* to help create a *new people* a little at a time, we'll get there. I

might not live to see this day, but with the help of all
of you, our people have grown in their understanding
—caring for others.

Dorothy was encouraged when she got a grant from a
group in Brasilia called PPG7, a group of seven countries
dedicated to ecology. That group gave awards for three-year
projects of reforestation. Since most of the farmers only
knew the "slash and burn" technique of farming, the more
workers who came, the more forest was lost. Dorothy was
seeing the devastation of the forest more and more each day.
She anguished over it. "So this magnificent Amazon forest
suffered year after year as they cut down another area of the
forest and burned it off. And they kept burning off more and
more. Then the big landowners began to arrive with cattle
and ranches and all this forest land was further degraded."
The population was increasing daily in Anapu and the politicians were seeing the town "developing."

While Dorothy and her community went about replanting
the forest as she had done in the past, the government was
awarding huge amounts of money to the big landowners
through a project called SUDAM (Superintendency for the
Development of the Amazon). Dorothy explained: "The government gave the big landowners $6M reais if they could come
up with a match of $6M reais. According to the agreement, the
landowners promised to reforest the area with coffee or asai [a
tropical fruit tree], but all they did was take the money and
now they are trying to show that they did other things with the
money to improve the land, but they really didn't." She noted
that Anapu had fifteen to eighteen of these projects and each
landowner had received $6M reais ($3 million). She said,
"The money would have been enough to take care of all the
small farmers who were beginning to get on their feet, but
no." Because of their desperate need, many of the small farmers took jobs with the landowners and had no time to plant
their own crops. "And over and above all this," she exclaimed,

"this project, SUDAM, was burning out our land in Anapu and we were going to INCRA day and night, because we were seeing our county being destroyed overnight."

The fight for land between the loggers and ranchers and the poor farmers began to intensify. The rural farmers had been awarded two huge areas of land to organize into land reserves. The tracts were on both sides of the Transamazon Highway where logging and ranching had been forbidden. Dorothy was going to Belém and Brasilia with her group, begging that the loggers' and ranchers' projects not be allowed in the reserves. She reported the many instances of illegal logging that she herself had observed as she visited the communities in the forest. She had seen the logging equipment in the forest and reported where it was hidden. She was able to name the loggers who were devastating the forest illegally and treating their workers like slaves. Because of her testimony, some of these loggers were fined heavily. She told of three men who worked for a logger and had reported being held at the worksite forcibly; how they had escaped by walking through the forest for three days without water or food until they came to a road and were picked up and brought to safety.

Very rarely did the federal police investigate. "However, with the millions left over from the project SUDAM, the big landowners paid lots of poor farmers to invade our reserves. We kept crying out that our reserve was being invaded." She said to the State Senate: "Have you ever heard a monkey sobbing in pain as his trees are being burned?" It was difficult for her to see that others did not share her passion for the restoration of the forest. Finally, she said, "INCRA named us as participants in the project called PDS, Project for Sustainable Development." Dorothy tells of a situation that was growing lethal.

In 2001, we hired two young agriculturalists from the university, paid by the Ministry of Environment, to help with the organization of our families living on

the reserve. On this reserve of land we ran into gunmen, hired by the ranchers. We regained control of
our land. We ran into gunmen again. We took back
our land and we held it. We got help from some
lawyers and the support of one fine politician, Ze
Geraldo, a state delegate, who helped us get defense
lawyers. And while we were working on this crisis,
the landowners organized the invasion of our reserve
on the other side of the Transamazon Highway.

Dorothy kept believing that there could be some way
that the government's help could be enlisted in stopping the
invasions of the reserves. In 2002 her community backed the
election of a mayoral candidate who had been proposed by
the group that had wanted to unite with them in the first
election. The community had agreed to work for him, since
he had told them that he was not tied to the ranchers, that
"we are all one," and that he was "with the people." He won,
along with the candidate from Dorothy's group who became
vice-mayor. But, within a few months, the mayor started
making comments about Dorothy, at one point referring to
her as "a scoundrel." In fact, in August, 2002, the federal police came to Anapu to investigate her.

One day, as she was walking down the street in Anapu, the
federal police picked her up for questioning. Fr. Amaro saw
them taking Sister Dorothy to the station and went home immediately to call the office of the state attorney general in
Belém. Fr. Amaro explained to the prosecuting attorney, Felício Pontes, that the federal police were questioning Dorothy
but no one knew exactly what was happening. Felício then
called the federal police in Belém and asked about what was
going on and who Dorothy's questioners were.

Dorothy describes what happened at the police station:

There was a knock on the door. One of the policemen stepped out of the room and when he came

back he said to me that Dr. Felício from the Attorney General's Office had said I was to tell the police
everything about the PDS project, because if I was
to be taken away as a prisoner, they had to take Felício himself first, since everything that I was doing
was under his direction. Our group had met with
Dr. Felício many times.

Hearing his message, I pulled out of my bag all
the maps and all the documents and they saw that
everything had been signed by INCRA or by IBAMA
or by the Attorney General's Office in Brasilia and
then locally by our organized groups and by our
politicians—our councilmen, our vice-mayor and
even our mayor. The police put all this information
into the computer.

Then came another knock on the door. One of
the policemen stepped out again. When he came back,
he told me that Dr. Felício said I was to tell the federal
police about the owner of the lumber company who
was stripping the forest and persecuting the people in
the area of land designated as a reserve. He said I was
to tell about everything that was happening there, to
give the name of the owner and to show documents
related to that owner, who did not have an authentic
forest permit—all his permits were false, forged. And
after that, the men in charge of my investigation called
Altamira and said that they could not proceed with the
investigation. Dr. Felício from the Attorney General's
Office defended me—what a great family! Felício is
wonderful. A new Brazil is his vision.

It was clear to Dorothy that the mayor of Anapu was
"selling out" her group, and this was proven during the next
election for mayor when he went against the poor farmers
and allied himself with the landowners. The group lost its

majority position in the County Council as well, because the mayor bought out the council members. The ranchers thought that Dorothy would be taken away in handcuffs, but then they heard that no charges would be brought against her. Investigators from the state police and the federal police realized that what she and her group were doing was all legal. It irritated the ranchers no end to hear that.

Dorothy was ecstatic when the progressive candidate, Luis Inácio Lula da Silva, was elected president in 2002. She wrote in a Christmas letter that year: "We just had national elections and our candidate won. He is Lula. He was a shoeshine boy—raised struggling and believing that a people united can bring change. We have walked together for years here dreaming of this possibility. Now all hands are on deck to make it happen. It has taken a long time."

But, unfortunately, within a few months her excitement was tempered by reality when Lula, facing a nearly bankrupt nation, proved unable to quickly enact the changes she had envisioned. She noted: "We have a new government trying to bring new life from so much corruption. But the old is still around...When we question injustices, some even ask if we are trying to tell people how to do things in Brazil as Bush tells the whole world. Power corrupts. Thank God St. Julie left us a strong heritage to be with the poor in their struggle for a more just existence." In fact, some of the ranchers spread the ludicrous rumor that Dorothy was President Bush's niece.

INCRA was trying to make the ecological reserve happen, but it was met with increased resistance. The landowners, now referred to by some as the "Wood Mafia," were organizing against INCRA, which had sent thirty cars in to support the efforts of the farmers in the reserve. The landowners held a *festa* and blocked the INCRA cars, paralyzing traffic. Dorothy called Dr. Felício to tell him about this and to inform him that there was an escalation of accusations against her and the farmers on the reserve.

The confrontations were growing ugly. Even on a privately owned radio station in Anapu, Dorothy was called a "troublemaker" and accused of interfering with the town's progress. In 2000, there had been about nine thousand people and two sawmills in Anapu. By 2004, there were approximately twenty-five thousand people and twenty-three sawmills. The loggers had streamed into the Anapu area after the southern part of the state of Pará had run out of lumber. Brazil was becoming the largest cattle exporter in the world. The logging business was booming and the exports were raising the economy of the country. President Lula tried to curb the destruction of the forest by suspending licenses to lumber companies. The organized loggers threatened to destroy roads and bridges and to pollute the water. Aware of their history of violence and brutality, the federal government backed down and logging resumed in earnest, on both legal and illegal land.

In September 2002 Dorothy shared in a letter to a friend: "Some of us are getting older and our presence in the woods is lessening due to physical demands of walking long distances in the forest where there are no types of roads—just jungle paths." She had turned seventy the previous year and had called it a "joyous moment," but she was aware that she was not as strong as she once had been. At the same time, she said,

> helping our people fight against logging firms and ruthless ranchers absorbs most of my time. I am here 20 years in this area Anapu. I know well who has land *documentos* and the false maneuvering done by government agencies. In our home we receive groups of men running to us from the woods. They have been threatened and their small families are asking for our support in facing the judicial processes thrown at them. We have at present some 500 to 600 families that have migrated this year to Anapu from areas that

have been depleted, areas where there is drought. Our road was improved and this is bringing these families.

Dorothy was the poor people's legal recourse. She was the one who knew the laws, the lawyers, and the government agencies to contact. The poor looked to her as their protector. But the government in the area had almost no power over the landowners, who paid off anyone who might get in their way and who hired gunmen to "clear the area." She knew that the odds against getting any kind of just settlement in a land dispute were against the poor, but she never stopped trying. Anapu and the surrounding area were being invaded by loggers and ranchers at an alarming rate. Greenpeace reported that, in 2002, fifty-three rural workers were killed in the Amazon and nineteen were killed in Pará; in 2003, seventy-three workers were killed, thirty-three of them in Pará. The situation was, in fact, getting worse.

Dorothy was very outspoken in her opposition to the loggers and ranchers who were against the sustainable forest project. There were nineteen illegal logging companies in the project area and continual threats were made against the rural farmers. A Greenpeace report stated that at least a third of the logging in the Amazon forest took place in Pará and only one percent of that was legal. A state four times the size of Germany, it had only seventy-two men dedicated to surveillance of illegal logging. To those who would rule by force, Dorothy was becoming an increasing nuisance.

The loggers and ranchers began to spread vicious rumors about Dorothy. They accused her of fomenting dissension among the poor. Some suggested that she was handing out guns to the farmers. For years, some people had called her a Communist, while others initiated a whispering campaign alleging that she was an agent for the United States government, which was planning to take over the Amazon and all its rich resources. A privately owned "scandal sheet" in Anapu called her a troublemaker and declared that she "needed to go." It was rumored that the mayor had openly stated, "We have to get rid of that woman if we are going to have peace." The board of Anapu declared her *persona non grata*. Her name appeared at the top of a published list of people with "bounties" on their heads. A reward of 50,000 reais ($20,000) awaited anyone willing to kill her.

Dorothy once said, "I know that they want to kill me, but I will not go away. My place is here alongside these people who are constantly humiliated by others who consider themselves powerful." She shared with a friend, "I have learned that faith sustains you and I have also learned that three things are difficult: as a woman, to be taken seriously in the struggle for land reform; to stay faithful to believing that these small groups of poor farmers will prevail in organizing and carrying their own agenda forward; and to have the courage to give your life in the struggle for change." However, she thought that being an American and being "an old woman" would protect her. She was wrong.

10

UNLESS A SEED DIE

During the summer of 2004, Dorothy had a welcome break from the mounting tensions in Anapu. Representing the Brazil unit of the Sisters of Notre Dame de Namur, she joined a special pilgrimage to France and Belgium on the occasion of the two-hundredth anniversary of the founding of the congregation. She loved being with other sisters and seeing the places where St. Julie had lived and worked among the poor. Dorothy saw the replica of the simple hut in Cuvilly, France, where Julie had lived, a place not too different from her home in Anapu. She prayed at the parish church of St. Eloi where Julie had prayed each day. It was located in the small village nestled among wheat fields that stretched out for miles around.

Julie's home had been attacked during an attempt on her father's life just before the French Revolution. Then, when the revolution broke out and Julie remained faithful to the Catholic Church, some of the revolutionaries wanted to kill her. She had to go into hiding for three years. Dorothy knew well what it was like to suffer death threats. She listened to the stories describing the many miles that Julie had walked to reach villages needing schools for the poor. Dorothy believed that Julie and she were kindred souls and she felt a special bond with her after that pilgrimage.

She returned to Ohio feeling renewed in spirit and affirmed in her work in Brazil. Some of her friends found her more pensive than before; she said she wanted to have more "God time" and often went to her room with a stack of tapes on spirituality and prayer. She commented to one sister, "I just want to sink myself in God." She was honest in sharing with the sisters that there were many in Brazil who wished her dead. A number of the sisters, as well as some of the members of her family, begged her to reconsider returning to Brazil, but she said that she did not want to abandon the struggle of these farmers who lived without any protection in the forest. "They have a sacrosanct right to aspire to a better life on land where they can live and work with dignity while respecting the environment," she said. She was grateful, too, that the leaders of the congregation were not forcing her to leave her beloved Amazon; they left the choice to her.

When she returned to Brazil, she first went to Brasilia with two men from Anapu to see the members of the new government. There she met with Nilmaro Miranda, the secretary for human rights, to tell him of the invasions by the ranchers and loggers and of the murders and intimidation going on. She wanted official documents showing that certain areas were, indeed, meant for the rural farmers and she asked that the government send the federal police to stop the gunmen and reaffirm the rights of the farmers to their land. In the previous two decades, over seven hundred murders had been committed in the state of Pará alone, and of those, only three had resulted in convictions. Dorothy was pleading for justice. She met with the heads of INCRA and IBAMA, and with the senator from Pará, Ana Julia Carepa. While the "heads of the new government" gave their support to the ideas in theory, little was done to assure the safety of the people. However, as she later wrote, there was one instance when the federal police *did* come to her area on August 20, 2004:

> Yesterday the federal police—IBAMA—environmental organ—made a blitz in Anapu and caught a *fazendeiro* (landowner) with 54 workmen cutting down our forest where INCRA (government agent for land reform) had given us a sustainable project in 1999 that has

never been able to begin. Always invaded. This time they had 24 chainsaws. Someone tipped me off. I had just gotten to Anapu Saturday, the 22nd, and Sunday they told me. I came fast to Altamira on Monday and IBAMA went right away on Wednesday—they had already cut 1000 hectares to the ground. Terrible destruction. The workers are all poor with no work —taking on any job to keep alive. We are in a bad way—more destruction each day and our mayor supports *big business*. "We shall overcome someday."

She continued to believe that the government would be able to stop the killings.

Samuel Clements, a twenty-four-year-old environmental student from England, and James Newton, a cameraman, had heard about Sister Dorothy. While they were in Brazil in 2003, they traveled north to see for themselves what she was doing and eventually made a film about her work. Sam vividly remembers his first meeting with Dorothy after his arrival in Altamira, how she burst through the door carrying a rose and startled him with a warm embrace. They became friends immediately. He describes his trip to Anapu the next day:

> We arrived in Anapu under the cover of darkness after a long, hot and bumpy bus ride. Sister Dorothy didn't want us to speak English, and if anyone asked questions, she would introduce us as her nephews. Mosquitoes buzzed incessantly.

The next morning, during their trip into the interior of the forest, Dorothy tried to point out the beauty of the land as well as areas of its devastation. However, she cautioned them to keep the camera hidden and to "keep low" when she showed them the burned-out regions of the forest. James attempted to capture the scenes on film. They also learned that the farmers were under the constant threat of gunmen and they had to be alert to danger. They went to a place near Esperança, deep in the forest. Sam describes what he saw:

> Before me rose a mighty rainforest, standing proud in the rich earth and deep sky. A delight to the senses. Sometimes we forget we are alive—we have to remind ourselves—but now I could not help but feel and celebrate every breath of life, its color, its richness. It was a place infinitely distant from anywhere I had previously been, yet so intimately close to something deep within.
>
> Behind lay the story of man's destruction, an unwinding yarn of degradation. A landscape raped and pillaged of life. The soil wept its worth into an aimlessly meandering steam stained with silt. A brown vein lost in a frail skin of endless pasture. The knowledge of what once existed there throbbed like a thorn in my side. Tears fell, but only to be caught by the dust that rose from the road, a road which ran like a scar through the forest.

The first night in the forest, they stayed with João Carlos,* a farmer who had been forced to move from his previous home by gunmen when his land was stolen by wealthy ranchers. He and his family, one of six hundred families receiving help from Dorothy's sustainable development project, had come to this part of the Amazon with the determination to stay. As Sam recalled, "Life seemed simple but hard. João showed us the stream in which to wash, whilst his wife cooked us rice and beans on a charcoal fire. Their chickens had produced only one egg that day. It was kindly shared among all eight of us."

---

*The name has been changed in order to protect the life of this farmer who is still threatened with invasion of his land.

When Dorothy took him to a meeting of the farmers, Sam saw the love the farmers had for her. He was both fascinated and saddened by the sight of the forest as well as by the stories of the people. Later, he said of Dorothy, "She had incredible energy, even though she was fighting incredible battles." His admiration of the seventy-two-year-old nun was boundless as he saw her champion the rights of the poor. The next year, on May 24, 2004, she wrote to Sam, telling him about João Carlos. "The situation sounded desperate," he recalled as he went on to quote from her letter: "Another shootout, this time at a place you visited. João Carlos and his wife were in the midst. His brother, who lived next door, had his home invaded by six hooded gunmen. He fled and I got out to Brasilia for help." Then she added, "The landowner is still a threat and these families are with others." Isolated in the forest with no means of communication with the "outside world," the farmers were vulnerable to attack without warning. The threat of invasion hung over them along with a gnawing fear that would not go away.

João Carlos was one of several farmers on the protected reserve accosted by these six hooded men with guns who threatened them with violence unless they left their land. The gunmen took their shoes, food, clothes, hoes, knives, and chickens. Ironically, they left the farmers' rifles, which they used for hunting game. The next day, the gunmen returned, but by now other farmers had arrived in support of their neighbors. A shootout ensued, leaving one of the hooded men dead. The police had shrugged their shoulders when told about the first invasion by the gunmen, ignoring the plight of the families who had lost everything. However, when the police heard about the shootout, they accused the farmers of planning an ambush. Some of the farmers had sought refuge in Dorothy's house, even though she was not there; it had become a symbol of safety. Later, she was accused of participating in the murder of the gunman.

In fact, Dorothy was in Brasilia at the time, once more pleading with federal government officials for protection for the farmers. She was asking them to do something to stop the wanton murders of her people and the destruction of the forest. She reminded them that the death of the forest would contribute to the destruction of much of the global environment. She found it so hard to believe that those who could help stop the killings were reluctant to do so. While her voice was soft, her steely blues eyes showed her resolve to do everything in her power to save the poor people she served. If that meant continually knocking on the doors of the legislators, then so be it. When she returned to Anapu, four of the men involved in the shootout were being held in jail without charge.

On October 9, Dorothy received a citation ordering her to appear in court on October 14 to hear the charges against her. She had been accused of aiding and abetting the farmers involved in the incident. It was rumored that Dorothy was responsible for starting an "armed rebellion" against the landowners and that she had been supplying guns to the farmers. All her life, Dorothy had taught nonviolence. The accusations were spurious and vindictive, as was obvious to all who knew her.

Sister Jane Dwyer and Sister Katy Webster accompanied Dorothy as she appeared before the judge for her hearing. When the defendants were introduced to the court, the judge was surprised to hear that the four men in jail had been beaten with iron rods and tortured. Dorothy was the first to be called to the stand. After being sworn in, Dorothy turned to the judge and said, "I don't know why I am here, but would you give me permission to pray, because God is here and will help us?"

The judge answered, "Certainly, Sister."

When the first question was put to her, Dorothy said that she needed to tell the judge the history of the land struggles going on, especially those having to do with the PDS project of sustainable farming land granted to the farmers by INCRA. For five hours, as she was questioned, Dorothy told one story after another of murder, theft, and the burning of houses taking place around Anapu, of the crops of the poor being destroyed, of cattle grass being sown among the farmers' rice or beans to choke their growth. At the end of the day, the judge thanked Dorothy and said that, after the accusers had been heard, she would be called back to the court. Dorothy did not live to attend the second session.

In the meantime, hundreds of letters were sent to the governor of the state of Pará defending Dorothy and saying that the very idea that she was organizing an armed revolt was absurd. She wrote to her sisters, who had sent many letters of support on her behalf: "I want to tell you of my deep gratitude for the tremendous support you gave to me and to the people of Anapu recently. This is a case where the voice of the poor cannot be heard because of the constant danger of assassination, but my belonging to an international congregation has made it possible for their voices not only to be heard but to receive a favorable response." Eventually, the four men were released from jail, two after three months and the other two after they had served sixteen months in prison.

When she returned to Anapu on October 28, Dorothy was asked to attend a meeting of farmers who had suffered an invasion of their village. Sister Joan sent a confidential e-mail, to the Sisters of Notre Dame only, informing them that she had received a message about Dorothy. In her e-mail she said, "When I called her, she was in a meeting with the people because one of the villages has been invaded by two ranchers and they took over 40 houses and have gunmen there so that the people cannot come back to their homes." The farmers had turned to Dorothy for help.

After the meeting, she returned to Altamira and spoke to the lawyers there about what the next steps should be. Eventually, INCRA confirmed that it had granted the land to the farmers, and that this land was part of the PDS reserve. The gunmen backed down and the farmers returned to their homes.

But the confrontations continued. While the politicians and landowners of Anapu were openly talking about "getting rid of that woman, Dorothy," she was being honored by the Brazilian Lawyers Organization for Human Rights, which bestowed on her its "Chico Mendes Medal" for 2004. On the back of the medal the inscription reads, "Honors heroes in the struggle for life and dignity." Her brother, David Stang, and her sister, Marguerite Stang Hohm, traveled to Belém to see their sister receive the honor on December 10, 2004. Sister Joan Krimm in Ohio commented, "Only in Brazil could one be accused of being a leader in organized crime and at the same time receive an award for humanitarian service." It seemed ironic that while Anapu had considered Dorothy *persona non grata*, she had received the "Honorary Citizen of Pará" award as well as having been named "Woman of the Year" by the Worker's Party at the legislature of the state of Pará in Belém.

David was aware of mounting tensions between the illegal loggers and landowners and his sister. He wrote in a Christmas letter, "The issue has become so volatile for Dorothy because the forest has been destroyed gradually and now the goons, killers, and illegal landowners have reached where Dorothy lives and wish to remove her." Her notoriety was obviously making her enemies nervous. David commented, "Being present [at the award ceremony] opened Marguerite's and my eyes to what an important focus Dorothy has now become. We saw her being interviewed on several TV stations and by several major newspapers in the city of over two million people. Being present was one enormous education for the two of us." In addition to witnessing the awards ceremony honoring Dorothy, David also saw senators, legislators, judges, and lawyers along with the poor people "looking at this 73 year old, white haired, soft spoken sister who has been awarded Brazilian citizenship, with hope, respect and love."

It was rumored and widely believed that, during January of 2005, a group of ranchers and loggers met at a secret, late night meeting in a hotel in Altamira to decide on how to get rid of Dorothy. She had become a "thorn in the side" of the landowners who wanted to increase their holdings. The markets for wood and cattle were expanding. She was exposing their illegal invasions of the reserves, which had already cost some heavy fines.

She herself had said:

> Today I receive open death threats from ranchers and grabbers of public lands. They have even dared threatening me and demanding that I be expelled from Anapu, only because I urge justice and friendship with the people, and I cherish their sincerity, willingness to share, hospitality, endurance, resolution and readiness. All I ask of God is His grace to help me keep on this journey, fighting for the people to have a more egalitarian life at all times and that we learn to respect God's creation.

Finally, two of the ranchers said that they would pay to have Dorothy killed. Vitalmiro Bastos de Moura, known as "Bida," has been identified both by the gunmen and their intermediary, Amair Feijoli da Cunha, known as "Tato," as being one of the instigators in the killing of Sister Dorothy; Regivaldo Pereira Galão, known as "Taradão," has been identified as the other. (The names of both men were on the "Dirty List" published by the federal government in the summer of 2006; they were identified as slave owners, with notations that they had been accused of ordering Dorothy's death.) Each one was alleged to have agreed to pay 25,000 reais (approximately $12,500) to hire someone to kill Dorothy. It is said that they attempted to hire a "professional assassin" who went to Anapu in January, but Dorothy was not there, so he stayed only a few days and, not wanting to be identified, left. Finally, the landowners made a deal with Tato, who worked for Bida, to get two of his workers to "do the job." The commission studying the assassination of Dorothy later concluded that there were more people involved in the plan than just the two men who were publicly identified.

Luis, a good friend of Dorothy's, was a leader in the small community of Boa Esperança. He had gathered the other farmers together to assure them that their land had been given to them by the government organization, INCRA. He knew that one of the ranchers, Bida, wanted to extend his ranch and take over their property, but Luis encouraged the farmers to stay on the land. On January 11, 2005, another e-mail to the sisters from Sister Joan stated, "I talked to Dot last night and she said things are getting more serious in Anapu. Yesterday, two more houses were burned in the area and weeds were sown in the fields these farmers had just planted. Today, a group of people are going into the area to occupy the existing houses so no more will be burned." Then she added, "This could turn out to be an explosive situation." Sister Joan wondered if this might be backlash because of the award Dorothy had received, and ended her e-mail by asking the sisters to pray that there would be no more violence.

One evening, shortly after this e-mail was sent, Luis heard the voices of three of Bida's men outside his shack. They had been drinking and were firing their guns in the air. They kept moving around his home, taunting him to "come out and fight like a man" and telling him that he had to leave. Luis had heard them do this before, but never had it been right at his house.

One of the gunmen, Tato, called out that he had bought the land from Bida and that it was his. Tato said that when he had bought the land, he did not know that Luis lived there. Tato had planned to build his own home on the site. Luis countered that he was on PDS land and had the right to live there. Tato insisted that the land was his and that if Luis and his family did not get out of their house by 6 AM the next morning, he would force them all out, line up his seven children, start with the youngest, and kill them all. Luis and his wife, Francisca, were terrified, since they knew that other houses had been burned. The three men outside kept drinking, shooting their guns, and laughing. Luis at one point asked them to "at least let us get some sleep," but they paid no attention to him. The children were frightened; the noise kept them all awake for most of the night. At 6 AM Tato was back, saying that it was time to leave and that they were going to burn down his house.

Luis asked for more time; Tato said that if they weren't out by nine o'clock, he and his men would burn down the house with them inside. Luis felt the anger welling up in him, but he knew that Tato was capable of doing something like what he was threatening, so Luis and his family gathered up their things and crossed the road. Tato, with a look of triumph, saw the parents and the terrified children carrying as much as they could into the forest, far enough to be hidden, but close enough to watch what the men were doing. The family looked on as Tato and the other two men poured gasoline around the house and torched it, laughing as it was reduced to ashes. Then they burned the crops that Luis had planted. Francisca and the children wept as they watched nearly all of what little they had being destroyed. The only place they had to go was deeper into the forest.

Bishop Erwin Krautler remembers the incident:

Luis told me his story and how he had suffered at the hands of Tato who persecuted, threatened and promised to kill him. Tato, Fogolo and Eduardo had made a hell for him and his family. It was a continual nightmare, many nights with no sleep and days lived in fear. However, on the day that Tato, with gun in hand, threatened to kill him and his family, "God set up a wall between him and us," Luis remembers, visibly shaken. "I felt the presence of God; God is always stronger than evil."

Dorothy heard of what had happened and went to find Luis and Francisca. She accompanied them to the police station in Anapu to report what had happened and pleaded with the police to do something about the crime, but the police seemed not to care. She showed them the map that clearly demonstrated that the area was a protected reserve, but the police said that they did not get involved in land disputes. Finally, Dorothy broke into tears. Luis and Francesca admitted that they were filled with fear for the other farmers.

Dorothy took Luis to Belém to talk to the people at INCRA. Once again she pleaded with them to do something about the violence and the impunity with which the gunmen got away with such crimes. She talked to members of the federal police, asking them for protection for the farmers. They promised to "do something" and agreed with her that she herself needed protection. They told her to ask for it the next time she went into the forest. She talked to Marina Silva, the minister for the environment, who sympathized with the farmers and also agreed that Dorothy and they should have protection. Dorothy was honest with Minister Silva about the many death threats that she had received and about those that had been reported to her. The minister responded that Dorothy *should* get protection and expressed concern for her safety.

Together with Luis, Dorothy set a date for a meeting on February 11 and 12 in Boa Esperança to encourage the farmers to stay on their land despite the threats and the actual violence they had suffered. Her map clearly showed that the farmers had a right to the land, since it was part of the PDS reserve for sustainable farming. Luis, in the meantime, had brought his family together to make a choice about their future. He asked them to decide whether they would leave their land and live in hiding or return home and build again. Francisca said, "Something inside of me remembered Dorothy's suffering and I said we should come back here. I made the choice to return in her name. I am here today for Dorothy."

The family returned to the place where their house had been. They were heartsick when they saw everything reduced to ashes. Many times, Dorothy had seen the farmers give up and leave an area to try to settle somewhere else. But she knew that this just gave the landowners more reason for frightening the farmers and strengthened their belief that they could get away with the intimidation. Until the farmers could establish themselves on protected land and have the government affirm their right to be there, the farmers would never have a place where they could live with dignity and safety. Dorothy made a mental note to take in blankets, food, and supplies for Luis and his family when she went to the meeting.

Before setting out for Boa Esperança, Dorothy went to Belém during the last week of January for some "spirituality days" with the other sisters in the area to celebrate the feast of the Presentation, a special feast for the Sisters of Notre Dame. During the days they were together, Dorothy seemed as happy and joyous as ever. She loved making pancakes for the community, having popcorn in the afternoon, and eating ice cream for dessert. However, when she stayed on after the rest had gone, Sister Jo Anne noticed that Dorothy looked tired and worried. Jo Anne even suggested that Dorothy stay on for a few more days, as it was getting close to Mardi Gras and the attention of most people would be fixed on that. But Dorothy told her she needed to go to a very important meeting with the farmers. They had been frightened by the burning of their houses, and she wanted to assure them of their right to be there. She asked Jo Anne to pray for her, as things were getting very tense in Anapu. Later she added, "Don't worry about my safety. The safety of the people is what's important." But Sister Jo Anne could not help but worry about Dorothy when she left.

In early February there was a symposium in Lima, Peru, for all the Sisters of Notre Dame serving in Latin America.

The administrative team for the whole congregation was there, along with many of the sisters serving in Brazil—Sisters Jane, who lived with Dorothy, Becky, Maria, Socorro, and Fatima. Sister Katy was in Itaituba attending an education meeting. That left only Nilda, the newest member of the congregation in Brazil, to go with Dorothy to the meeting in Boa Esperança. Fr. Amaro, Dorothy's strong supporter and good friend, invited Dorothy to accompany him to a meeting for parish ministers, but she insisted on going to the gathering in the forest. She assured the sisters and Fr. Amaro that the police in Anapu had promised her protection. Still, it was disconcerting to learn that Tato had been seen frequently at the police station that week.

Nilda, who had entered the congregation in Brazil only three months earlier, had just moved in with Dorothy and was getting accustomed to life in Anapu. One day, she asked Dorothy how she prayed. Dorothy answered, "Nilda, I light a candle, I look at Jesus carrying his cross, and I ask for the strength to carry the suffering of the people." Nilda was struck by those words; they were to become even more important in the days that followed.

On the morning of February 11, Dorothy called her brother, David, in Palmer Lake, Colorado. She said, "Just hearing your voice makes me feel the cool fresh air of Palmer Lake even though it is so hot and humid here in Anapu." He answered that it was 4 AM in Colorado and wondered about her call. After sharing with him that she was worried about the meeting and that she felt it might be dangerous, she added, "This is going to be a tough one," and asked for his prayers. Then she said, "I can't talk long because there are people outside my door asking me to go down the road with them to show support for several poor families who had their crops and houses burned down by hired hoodlums." David was concerned; his sister didn't sound like her herself. He had a feeling something was terribly wrong.

Later, Dorothy made breakfast for Nilda and those going with her to Esperança. She hurried to prepare the pancakes for

Ivan, their driver, and Gabriel, the vice-president of the Farmers' Union, who had agreed to go with her. She knew it was a good three- or four-hour trip, but it could be even longer if the rains came and the road became treacherous. At about eight o'clock, she announced that she wanted to go to the police station to see who was going with them. Ivan said he would take her in the Farmers' Union truck. When they arrived at the station and asked who would be going, the policeman said, "Oh, we're sorry, Sister, but we can't send anyone today because we have had trouble with our car." Dorothy assured them that a police officer could come with them in the union's truck, but he answered, "Sister, you are supposed to know a lot about the law, but you obviously don't know that we have a law that says we cannot ride in anyone's private vehicle." Besides, he added, "the people are safe." Stunned, Dorothy left the police station only to see the police car being driven down the road. As usual, she and the people were going to be on their own.

Upon leaving the station, Dorothy, looking very disturbed, asked Ivan if he felt fearful. He answered that he didn't, believing that no one would hurt her. But Ivan could see that there was something on her mind. They returned to the house in Anapu to load up the truck with the blankets, plants, and food supplies for the farmers whose homes had been burned. Dorothy seemed especially quiet on the long journey into the interior. Her usual happy smile and excitement were replaced by a pensive gaze out the window as they passed the wide, flat pasture lands that had replaced the forest. At one point Dorothy finally said, "If something is going to happen, I hope it happens to me, because the others have families to care for." Ivan experienced a sense of foreboding that he had not had before.

The group arrived at about 3:30 PM and found several farmers waiting for them. They all went to the place where a community center was being constructed. Tato and his men, Raifran and Clodoaldo, had chopped up the wood the farmers had planned to use to build a project coordination center. Raifran and Clodoaldo had been clearing some of the land to make a shelter for themselves. The two of them were sitting on a log outside the meeting space. Dorothy and a group of people approached them and asked them to put off any building until after the meeting, when the ownership of the lot in question would be settled. Raifran and Clodoaldo agreed to wait a while. Dorothy invited them to the meeting with Reginaldo, the agricultural technician, who was going to talk that afternoon about planting cação beans, a potential cash crop. They declined to attend. Instead, they sat outside with Tato, and watched and listened.

The climate was tense. The people already considered Tato a terrorist, and there he was with two other men, standing around and watching the people. Gabriel thought that he should go talk to them. Knowing that Tato despised Dorothy, Gabriel took the lead, explaining why they had come and inviting Tato to the meeting the next morning to discuss the ownership of the land. Dorothy tried to explain that because it was PDS land, the farmers were planning to build a center there.

Suddenly, Tato exploded in fury. He declared that no one was to enter the area. He turned to Dorothy and spat out the words, "I don't owe you anything. I bought this land and I intend to get these people off of it." Gabriel thought the situation could turn violent. He and Dorothy retreated for the time being but later tried again to have a conversation with him. This time Tato told Dorothy that if anyone attempted to build on his land he would take action. Then he added, "Listen, Sister, you aren't going to have the strength to carry all the dead people out of here." Dorothy did not reply. She still hoped that she could convince him that the land was a preserve of INCRA. After the meeting, they divided themselves up and went to different houses for the evening.

Dorothy, Nilda, and Ivan went to Maria's house and found Vicente there as well. Vicente had two buildings and offered Dorothy his second house for the night. Maria wanted Dorothy to stay with her as she had originally intended to do. But Vicente insisted that he had room for Dorothy and said he wanted her to come to his place for dinner. She accepted his invitation. Everyone there knew Raifran and Clodoaldo, but Vicente knew them best. Dorothy may have thought that if she could talk to Vicente and show him the map of the PDS, he could influence the other two men.

That evening, they heard the car with Tato, Raifran, and Clodoaldo go by. Later it would be parked in the middle of the road. Tato told Gabriel that their battery was giving them trouble. When they had tried to push the car, he said, they were unable to do so because of the mud, and so they had left it blocking the road. Strangely, there was a tree across the only other road, meaning that both exits out of Esperança were blocked.

The plan to kill Dorothy had actually been finalized only the day before. Tato had asked Clodoaldo if he was interested in making some money. When Clodoaldo said he was, Tato told him of Bida's proposition. Whoever had the courage to kill Dorothy would get 50,000 reais ($25,000). When Clodoaldo said he was willing to do this, Tato handed him a .38 caliber pistol. Quoting Regivaldo Galvao, the other rancher involved in the plot, who had said that until they got rid of "that nun," they would have no peace, Bida had told Tato that there would probably be a fuss for a few days, but then things would calm down as they usually did.

Clodoaldo presented the plan to Raifran. The two men spoke for a while and finally agreed that they would do it together. It was more money than either man had ever seen, and besides, they reasoned, it was easy to get away with murder where they were; lots of other people did. Clodoaldo talked Raifran into being the one to use the gun.

Later, the two gunmen admitted that it had been their intent to kill Dorothy that night, as she slept at Vicente's house. They had planned to kill her and then return to their shelter and meld with the crowd the next morning, pretending to be shocked at the murder of the nun. But when they came to Vicente's and looked through the slats at the side of the house, they could not see Dorothy. They expected to see her in a hammock. But she had spent the night sleeping on the dirt floor.

The rain was steady and the night was turning cold. Somewhere in a dingy bar in Anapu late that Friday night an old man was drinking heavily and said in a voice loud enough for some of the farmers to hear, "I wonder if that old woman is dead yet."

11

A SEED PLANTED

It was raining softly the next morning, and the cool of the night was gradually giving way to a humid haze. Dorothy rose early, wanting to be at the meeting place when the people arrived. Raifran and Clodoaldo were watching for her and saw her speaking to someone around seven-thirty. When she finished the conversation, Dorothy started up the narrow path to the community center. Passing Cicero's house, she called to him to ask him to go with her. Cicero called back that he wasn't quite ready, but that she could go on ahead and he would catch up with her.

At the top of a small hill Dorothy found herself surrounded by a canopy of magnificent trees. At that moment Raifran and Clodoaldo stepped out in front of her, blocking her path. Dorothy greeted them kindly and began to discuss with them the "rights of the earth," telling them that they should not plant cattle grass because it harms the environment. She spoke about preserving the forest and told them that she understood their position, that they were soldiers who had been given "orders."

In the meantime, Cicero had set out after Dorothy and was about ten minutes behind her. When he saw that the two men had blocked her path, he hid in the bushes and watched to see what would happen. At one point, she removed the map from her plastic shoulder bag, crouched down, unfolded the map, and spread it out on the ground to show them the delineation of the areas for the PDS. Raifran turned to Clodoaldo, who was seated on a stump, and looked for the signal to shoot, but Clodoaldo shook his head no. Dorothy stood up again. Raifran asked if she had a weapon. She answered that the only weapon she had was her Bible, which she immediately produced from her bag. She read a passage about how God left all things for everyone to use, and then she read from the Beatitudes: "Blessed are the poor in spirit, for theirs is the kingdom of heaven; blessed are those who hunger and thirst for justice, for they shall be filled; blessed are the peacemakers, for they shall be called children of God."

As she finished reading these lines, Raifran turned once more to get Clodoaldo's permission to fire, but again he shook his head. She invited them to come to the meeting at the community center and then said, "God bless you, my sons," turned, and started walking away. Raifran drew the revolver from his belt, looked over at Clodoaldo, and again awaited the signal. This time Clodoaldo nodded his head.

"Sister," he called after her. Dorothy turned, and she saw the gun. Raifran spoke: "If you haven't solved this problem till now, you're not going to be around to solve it any longer." She raised her hand, still holding her Bible, as if to shield herself, and Raifran fired. The first bullet passed through her hand before lodging in her abdomen. Dorothy fell face down on the ground. As Clodoaldo ran into the bushes, Raifran moved in closer and shot again. This time the bullet penetrated her shoulder from the back. Then he moved right up to her head and fired four more times, emptying his gun before he too ran.

As the rain continued coming down, Dorothy lay bleeding on the ground. Cicero ran behind the houses to Maria's house yelling, "They've shot Sister Dorothy! They've shot Sister Dorothy." He knew the gunmen must have seen him, and he was afraid for his own life. Everyone was terrified. Fearing that the gunmen might come after the other sister and kill her as well, Ivan told Nilda to get into his truck and then started driving. He had to cut away the log blocking one of the roads so that he could get Nilda out of the area. Once he had gotten her to a safe place, he left his truck there for fear that the gunmen might destroy it, and walked back to Esperança.

Two children found Gabriel and yelled, "Gabriel! Dot's been shot!" Gabriel and Luis rushed to where Dorothy was lying, hoping they could save her. As they hurried up the hill, Gabriel saw Tato in the distance, but he didn't see the gunmen. No one knew what to expect next; Tato had been so threatening the night before. The farmers feared that the gunmen were going to come after all of them.

When Gabriel and Luis reached the spot where Dorothy had been shot, they found her lying on her side, the rain washing her blood into the mud. Her hand was to her mouth, as if she were biting her finger in pain. Gabriel searched for a pulse and was the first to discover that Dorothy was dead.

The farmers were in shock; they couldn't believe that anyone would actually kill her. Quickly they returned to the houses where the people were gathering, struggling to cope with what had happened. People were crying. No one was clear on what they should do. There was no escape and the gunmen were on the loose, somewhere in the area.

On the way back to Esperança, Ivan asked Reginaldo to go to Anapu on his motorcycle and notify the police. Having seen Dorothy's body and knowing how she had died, Ivan was concerned that Cicero be protected, as he was the only witness to the murder. Nobody knew where Raifran and Clodoaldo were hiding and everyone felt very vulnerable. Within a short time, they smelled something burning. Someone had torched Tato's car after retrieving Raifran's identification papers from it. When the fire died down, they moved the car off the road.

All day, Dorothy's body lay on the ground with the rain washing over her. People huddled together in their houses in fear and in sorrow. They kept straining to hear the sound of the police coming; the wait seemed like an eternity. People were afraid to go near Dorothy's body because they expected the gunmen to return. Then, at about 4 PM, they heard a helicopter hovering over the spot where Dorothy had been murdered. Although Dorothy's good friend, Marina Silva, the minister for the environment, was trying to get to her, the pilot could not see through the lush, green, majestic trees that Dorothy had loved so much. This is where Dorothy loved to be, in the midst of the forest still virgin in its beauty, still untouched by the destruction threatening its existence. She had tried so hard to save it, but she had been crushed by the same greed that was destroying her beloved forest and the people of the Amazon.

When Reginaldo reached Anapu, he had a hard time convincing the police to come to Esperança to retrieve Dorothy's body. They said they did not have a car to go into the forest, that it was raining, and besides, the police car was busy with other things. Only when Reginaldo said that then the farmers would drive her body out did the police decide that maybe they should go. They left in a farmer's truck, even though the previous morning they had said they could not travel in a private vehicle. They did not reach the settlement until late that afternoon.

By five o'clock, Ivan had decided that the police weren't coming and that he would drive Dorothy's body back to town himself. He could not stand the thought of her body lying in the rain and dirt all night. But, just at that moment, the police arrived and forbade anyone to touch her. Gabriel's anger flared and he said to them, "We asked for protection for her when she was alive. Now we don't need it for a cadaver on the ground." The police demanded that he accompany them back to Anapu to give an account of what had happened, but Gabriel said he wanted to stay with Ivan and Cicero and to make sure the farmers were all right before he left.

In the meantime, news of Dorothy's murder had reached President Lula. He immediately ordered the federal police, who were with Marina Silva, to go to the crime scene to prevent more violence. As soon as Marina's helicopter landed in

Anapu, the federal police were sent to Esperança to secure evidence and protect any witnesses. They retrieved Dorothy's plastic bag with her Bible, maps, and other documents. And, finally, they put Dorothy's body in the back of the farmer's truck and took her back to the hospital in Anapu.

By that evening Reuters News Service had picked up the story and the news was quickly spreading. Gabriel, Ivan, and Cicero arrived back in Anapu just before midnight. When Gabriel got to his house, he found a large crowd of people waiting for him, wanting to know what had happened. All of them were in a state of shock; most were in tears.

Not everyone shared their grief. As word spread around Anapu, some people set off firecrackers to celebrate the fact that Dorothy was dead. A few of the locals chided the farmers, saying, "That's what you get" or "The same thing will happen to you." The old man who had wondered whether Dorothy was dead the night before went to the bar on Saturday evening and mocked the farmers saying, "So you have lost your *madre*, have you? Who will protect you now?" A few days after the murder, a note was shoved under Gabriel's door at the Farmers' Union with the message, "Gabriel, if you really love your children, you won't let them out of your sight." There was widespread fear among the farmers that more people would be killed.

By Tuesday, two thousand troops had been flown into the area to establish peace and prevent any more violence. Helicopters hovered over the town as the troops expanded their hunt for the murderers. They were under pressure to resolve the case. The Brazilian secretary for human rights, Nilmaro Miranda, said publicly, "Solving this crime and apprehending those who ordered and committed it is a question of honor for us. This is intolerable." The federal police worked with their civilian counterparts and insisted that they find those responsible. The town seemed to be under a state of siege.

When Sister Inez and Sister Benedicta, two Franciscan sisters in Altamira who were good friends of Dorothy's, received the news of her death, they immediately set off for Anapu to protect her house and to be with Nilda, who was alone. They were bombarded with phone calls and people coming by to hear what had happened. They had been told that Dorothy's body had been taken to the municipal hospital in town. But the hospital in Anapu did not have a morgue and, in a case of murder, the police needed an autopsy done. As a result, by early the Sunday morning the police had arranged for a Brazilian Air Force plane to fly Dorothy's body to Belém. By this time, the story of Dorothy's murder was being reported on every evening news channel in Brazil, and the story quickly circled the globe. From as far away as China, Rumania, Iraq, and Kenya, tens of millions of people were hearing about a simple nun who had worked in Brazil for nearly forty years and who had been gunned down because of her work for the poor people in the Amazon. Brazilians of all classes were shocked and ashamed that this could have happened in their country.

Because of the storms on Sunday morning, the plane carrying Dorothy's body did not arrive in Belém until after 4 PM. A crowd of people had gathered outside the medical building where the morgue was located to wait for Dorothy to arrive. They had been standing there since early morning. Overnight, in an amazing show of support and as an expression of outrage, protest, and solidarity with Dorothy's work, members of the Conference for Religious of Brazil, representatives from the National Conference of Brazilian Bishops, the popular movements, human rights groups, lawyers, Notre Dame associates and friends joined with the people waiting at the medical building in Belém. They carried banners demanding justice for her murder and chanted *"Dorothy Vive!"* over and over again.

Sister Jo Anne Depweg made her way to the medical building and joined those waiting while she tried to absorb what she had heard. Finally, the van carrying the coffin appeared, surrounded by a police escort with lights flashing.

Sister Jo Anne reported, "Dorothy was welcomed by the crowd with warm applause, chants, and so much affection." Everyone shouted, "*Dorothy Vive!*" People allowed Sister Jo Anne to move toward the door as the van backed up to the building. She wept uncontrollably. With her hand on the van as if trying to steady it, the realization that her good friend Dorothy had truly been murdered began to sink in. Suddenly, someone was asking her to "identify the body." At that point, more Sisters of Notre Dame, Ani Wihbey, Rita Raboin, and Betsy Flynn from São Luis appeared and were ushered into the room where Dorothy's body was lying on an examining table. The horror of the news and the reality of the murder struck all of them more profoundly when they saw her lying there. It was no longer just a bad dream. It was the first time since they had heard the news that they were together and they were able to share their sorrow with one another. The crowd outside was singing and praying, giving testimonies about Sister Dorothy and voicing their demand for justice. Makeshift banners were held high. Bishop Xavier, who had known Dorothy when he was a young priest, was waiting in the crowd, along with another good friend of hers, Pastor Marga Rothe, a Lutheran minister.

Only Sister Ani, who had a nursing background, was allowed to remain with the physician during the autopsy. When it was finished, the sisters were ushered back into the room to see Dorothy and be with her for what proved to be a very short private time. Sister Jo Anne had brought Dorothy's favorite dress with her. Dorothy had loved that dress because the material was patterned with sunflowers, the symbols of the Sisters of Notre Dame. St. Julie had said, "You must turn to God like the sunflowers always turn to the sun."

When they dressed Dorothy, they noticed that her body was still very supple and they surmised that the many hours of lying in the rain may have helped to preserve her body for awhile. They were horrified to see so many gunshots in her and wondered if she had felt much pain. They were comforted by the fact that her face seemed peaceful and serene, almost as if she were smiling. The bullets had entered the back of her head and had not marred her face.

The sisters were able to talk to Dorothy, telling her of their love. They had time to cry and hold each other, time to pray with Dorothy and say their good-byes. Then they sang some of her favorite songs. It was all too soon that other people came into the room and asked them to leave, as the mortuary had orders to take Dorothy to the church of St. Maria Goretti, the parish church near the home of the Sisters of Notre Dame in Belém, in the district of Guama.

A slow, solemn procession of cars wound its way to the church. It arrived at about 10:00 PM and found another large crowd of people waiting for Dorothy. Her coffin was draped with the flag of Brazil. People were carrying flowers and lighted candles, wanting so hard to do something to express their love. The sisters had preceded Dorothy's body and were there to receive her when she arrived at the church. Bishop Flavio of Abaetatuba, Bishop Carlos, newly elected bishop of Castanhal, and Bishop Xavier of Maranhão and five other priests from the area, including Fr. Bruno, the pastor, concelebrated a Mass. The people of Guama had prepared the whole service while the sisters were at the medical building. The liturgy was simple and dignified, worthy of Dorothy "in her greatness and humility." The Lutheran minister, Marga Rothe, gave a beautiful eulogy, passionately pleading for justice and an end to impunity in the state of Pará. When she finished, she received an overwhelming ovation from the congregation gathered in the church. As the Mass was taking place, Bishop Orani, the new archbishop of Belém, who had been traveling and had just arrived from the airport, came into the church to be with the people. At the end of Mass, he rose from his seat in the pews and apologized for not being there for the liturgy. Then he invited everyone to return for a 4:30 AM Mass the next morning which he would celebrate for Dorothy. After an all-night vigil in the church filled with people, hundreds more appeared the next morning to bid Dorothy their final farewell. Bishop Xavier joined the archbishop and three other priests in concelebrating the morning liturgy. Pastor Marga was invited to be with them. Sister Jo Anne commented, "Dorothy would have been very happy to see her there!"

The sisters describe what happened next:

> Afterwards, we all left for the airport to accompany Dorothy back to where she lived and worked in the prelacy of Xingu. Many sisters of the Conference of Religious accompanied us in order to bid their final farewell to Dorothy and to wish us a safe trip. The two planes left at 7 AM. Marga, Rita, Betsy, and Sandra were privileged to have Dorothy's body resting at their feet in the back of the plane.

Sisters Katy, Raminha, Lu, and Josi arrived in Altamira from Itaituba. Sister Mary Alice McCabe and Fr. Nello had arrived the day before to help plan the Mass there.

Hundreds of people had gathered in the church in Altamira to greet Dorothy. Bishop Xavier, who had come in one of the planes, joined Bishop Erwin Krautler of the Xingu prelacy in celebrating a Mass for her. Again, Pastor Marga was invited into the sanctuary.

After lunch, the sisters and those with them boarded the planes to Anapu. This time there were five small planes and one larger one with the coffin. The government had provided the larger plane, since it did not want people lining the route along the Transamazon Highway; the threat of violence was too great. When the planes landed on the small area of asphalt in Anapu, cars were ready to take the coffin, the sisters, and a number of government officials to St. Lucy's, Dorothy's home parish. But before getting into the cars, the sisters met Fr. Amaro, Ivan, Gabriel, and many other friends of Dorothy's for the first time. These friends needed to tell the sisters how much they loved Dorothy; they wanted to cry with them and hug them. They wanted to thank the community of Notre Dame for having given Dorothy to them. The sisters were touched by the love poured out for one of their own. They were impressed that Dorothy had touched so many people, more than they would ever know. Her coffin was placed in a van and taken to St. Lucy's Church where she had prayed so often. Hundreds of people came to pay their respects throughout the all-night vigil.

For the next morning, Fr. Amaro, the pastor of St. Lucy's, and many of his parishioners had organized a Mass of Christian Burial at the community center near São Rafael where Dorothy was to be buried. She had requested that she be buried in the Amazon forest near where her people lived. Twenty-seven people had traveled from Belém in an extraordinary gesture of solidarity. They were mostly young people who had caught from Sister Dorothy the fire of passion for service and work for justice. They had raised the money themselves to pay for their tickets; they just wanted to be there for her last moments. Now they joined the other mourners as the flag-draped coffin was carried on the shoulders of six men from the church.

A procession of over two thousand people accompanyied Dorothy to the center. Giomar and his two sons, who owned the land near São Rafael, had built a swinging bridge across the Anapu River that the whole procession crossed into the forest area. Government officials, Marina Silva, minister for the environment, Nilmaro Miranda, secretary for human rights, Senator Ana Julia Carepa, Felício Pontes, federal public prosecutor for the state of Pará, and many other government officials were among the people honoring Dorothy that day. Reporters from all over the world were also there to interview farmers and government officials. TV crews darted in and out of the procession line, getting background shots and capturing the moment to show on national and international stations.

The people came singing, praying, and carrying banners extolling Dorothy and demanding justice for her murder.

Many had come from the interior of the forest, some walking twenty miles in the rain and mud to be there. Some had come long distances on crutches; others carried newborns. A circle of small children, each holding a large, yellow "cloth" petal attached to a brown circular center representing a sunflower, would occasionally stop and move around in a circle, singing a song for Dorothy. Simple farmers, many covered with the red, relentless mud that blankets everything during the rainy season, needed to be with Dorothy as they laid her to rest. They carried candles and flowers. Some were on bicycles, some on motorcycles. They stood singing and praying, the silence broken often by the sobs of those who simply had to let their feelings spill over. Along the route of the procession, soldiers stood by with guns ready, offering protection for the people. It was a protest march, it was a celebration of her life, it was a sorrowful funeral procession for someone who was dearly loved and who had offered her life to bring justice to a violent land.

Bishop Xavier was there again, having followed Dorothy from Belém to her final resting place. Bishop Erwin Krautler had come as well, and together with Fr. Amaro and several other priests gathered to prepare for the Mass. Once again they invited Pastor Marga to join them on the stage set up for the celebration. Then they asked Sister Jo Anne to say something before they began the liturgy.

After welcoming the people on behalf of the Sisters of Notre Dame, Sister Jo Anne remembered something that a farmer had said to her the night before at the vigil at St. Lucy's Church. She wanted to share the thought with everyone. She said, "Today, we are not going to *bury* Dorothy, we are going to *plant* her." Then she raised her hands high and called out, "*Dorothy Vive!*" and all shouted over and over, "*Dorothy Vive!*"

The Mass was beautiful, the singing glorious, and the people prayerful and reverent. But right in the middle of the celebration, Bishop Erwin stopped the Mass long enough to announce that a Farmers' Union leader in the south of Pará had just been murdered. The crowd groaned audibly and more tears were shed. The general feeling of "when will the killings stop?" prevailed for a few minutes until the bishop resumed the Mass. When the celebration was over, the pallbearers once again lifted Dorothy's coffin onto their shoulders.

When they reached the simple grave dug in the dirt, they gently placed the coffin beside it until most of the crowd had gathered. They prayed again for Dorothy and then lowered the casket into the grave. Many people moved forward to throw some dirt on the coffin, others to throw their flowers into the grave. Finally, several men took shovels and covered the coffin with earth. When they were finished, people placed their candles on top of grave. Soon, there were hundreds of lighted candles shining from Dorothy's final resting place. It was a fitting symbol for someone who had been a light to hundreds of people suffering from the darkness of hate and oppression. The grave was ablaze with light.

The next two days were hectic for the Sisters of Notre Dame in town. The phone calls were relentless. Reporters wanted more information, people wanted to express their sympathy and share their sense of loss. It was a swirl of emotions for everyone. The helicopters kept buzzing overhead as the jungle troops searched for the killers. It was difficult for anyone to have time for grieving and rest.

Those who thought that Sister Dorothy would be silenced by her murder were badly mistaken. The story of a seventy-three-year-old American nun who was shot while trying to bring justice to the poor in the Amazon and who was championing sustainable farming there to save the forest from destruction caught the imagination of the press, and it quickly spread worldwide. Dorothy's story touched a nerve, jolting the complacent and exposing the ignorance of most people about the violence and destruction that was going on in the Amazon. For weeks, the Ohio provincial, Sister Elizabeth Bowyer, and Sister Joan Krimm were on the phone, sometimes for ten hours a day, answering the questions of reporters from all over the world.

Memorial services were held across the United States, sometimes in the schools and parishes served by the Sisters of Notre Dame, but just as often in other places. Dorothy, who had been little known in her lifetime, was suddenly thrust into the world's consciousness. Greenpeace, the environmental organization that had for years been trying to tell the public about the destruction of the Amazon region, broadcast extensive news of the murder. Peace organizations honored and extolled Dorothy for all she had done in the face of such violence. Amnesty International wrote a scathing letter to the Brazilian government, denouncing the impunity with which so many people got away with murdering the landless poor. Religious leaders acknowledged that Dorothy was truly a martyr, whose life modeled the call of all believers who long for justice. Whether religious or secular, millions recognized the courage of a single woman who had attempted to save the lives of the poor and give them some freedom and dignity. And in Brazil, the account of Dorothy's death became a rallying cry for those who were working among the poor. In the months after her murder, Dorothy would be lavished with honors and praise.

The Sisters of Notre Dame continued to present Dorothy's story as a model of the mission of the congregation, to become "Women with Hearts as Wide as the World." They did not want the plight of the poor farmers in the Amazon to be forgotten. They were determined to raise awareness wherever they could of the dangers to the environment resulting from the destruction of the Amazon. They would continue to hear inspiring stories about the people whose lives Dorothy had touched.

One story involved her brother, David. While visiting Anapu after his sister's death, David was sitting with the sisters in their home when suddenly a man came to the door. Those from Anapu were immediately cautious, as this man and his family had been opposed to the Catholics in the town. But the man asked which of them was Dorothy's brother and, when David identified himself, the man went over to him, threw his arms around him, and wept. After he had composed himself, the man told the story of his brother who had worked with him in running two small shops in town. One day, his brother, with a truck loaded with goods for the store, was stopped on the road by three strangers. They dragged him out of his truck and began beating him mercilessly. Suddenly, another "stranger" drove up in an old Volkswagen, jumped out of the car and startled the three thieves so that they ran to their car and left. The "stranger" was Dorothy. She put the injured man in her car and drove him to the hospital where she stayed with him until he died. The man had come simply to thank David for his sister's care and bravery. David had never heard the story before.

Some of the stories had the makings of legend. One of them was told by Sister Mary Alice McCabe who works in the State of Ceara with poor fishermen. For two years, the fishermen had gone out to catch lobsters, but the waters were polluted and their catch was meager. As they lamented their losses, since this was their only source of income, they made a decision. They would get together to buy an old boat, fix it up, and call it "The Dorothy." When they took her out for her first run, they came back with over one hundred and fifty pounds of lobsters, the largest catch they had had in years. They were ecstatic. And the stories continue.

While her body rests in Anapu near the forest she loved so much, Dorothy's spirit continues to animate the people she served. When hundreds of people gathered in St. Lucy's Church on February 12, 2006, the first anniversary of her murder, the resounding shouts of *Dorothy Vive!* rose again and again as the crowd came together to celebrate Mass. Following the service, the congregation processed once more to Dorothy's gravesite where Greenpeace and dozens of volunteers had pounded 820 white crosses into the ground. Each cross represented either someone who had been murdered for working for justice or a poor farmer who had been killed in the Amazon during the last twenty years. In addition, there were seventy-two red crosses, representing those who had recently received death threats because of land conflicts. In the year following Dorothy's murder, eighteen more people were killed in the state of Pará. While the killing has not stopped, the determination of the poor farmers has been strengthened to work for their rights and to keep hope alive. Their self-esteem has grown and their resolve to keep the base ecclesial communities going, to share with each other and to grow in their understanding of the Bible, is alive and well.

As the women circled the grave and held hands that day, Antonia, a leader in the women's movement, spoke to Dorothy. She promised on their behalf to continue the struggle for social justice and to work for peace, to defend human rights, and to challenge society to search within itself for faith and strength to continue what Dorothy had begun. She expressed the feelings of all those gathered when she said, "Dorothy, we promise to continue using your smile and your faith every day in our struggle, and to continue planting the seeds of love, peace and social justice."

Clearly they were expressing a profound truth when the crowd responded: "*Dorothy Vive!*" Dorothy lives.

EPILOGUE

After Dorothy's murder on Saturday, February 12, President Luiz Inácio Lula da Silva sent 110 soldiers of the Fifty-first Jungle Infantry Division to Anapu by helicopter to maintain order. The following Tuesday, two thousand more troops were sent into the State of Pará. The military police were to work with their civilian counterparts to capture the suspects in the murder, as well as to prevent further violence. Even all this was not enough to prevent the murder of three other Brazilian activists working for land reform during the week following Dorothy's death.

On February 13, the attorney-general of the Republic, the national land ombudsman, and the president of INCRA traveled to the state of Pará in order to help with the investigations. The witnesses from Esperança knew exactly who had pulled the trigger to silence Dorothy once and for all. The justice of the state of Pará issued an order of preventive arrest for four people suspected of being involved in Dorothy's assassination, namely, the two gunmen, the person who ordered the murder, and the one who was the intermediary between them.

On February 14, 2005, President Lula announced the creation of two new national parks in the Amazon rain forest and expanded another to preserve an environmentally sensitive region next to a proposed road. Late that Monday evening, the president signed a decree placing nearly eight and a half million acres of the Amazon forest under federal environmental protection and suspended logging in some hotly contested areas. The land was being reclaimed for the peasant farmers for sustainable farming. The reclamation project was designated "Project Dorothy Stang."

By February 19, Amair Frejoli da Cunha, known as "Tato," presented himself to the Police Station Specializing in Crimes against Women in Altamira. Accompanied by his lawyer, Tato acknowledged that he knew the rancher who had ordered the murder, but said that he himself had nothing to do with it. He was arrested and put in jail.

On February 20, Raifran das Neves Sales was simply walking down a road when someone recognized who he was and notified the police. Shortly afterwards, he was arrested. The next day, the federal police arrested Clodoaldo Carlos Batista, who was charged with being Dorothy's second executioner.

Vitalmiro Bastos de Moura, known as "Bida," accompanied by his lawyer, surrendered to the police on March 27, 2005. By April 27, Regivaldo Pereira Galvão had also been arrested, although he denied having anything to do with the killing.

Hundreds of petitions were sent to the federal government in Brasilia asking that those involved in the crime be tried in a federal court. Because so much impunity had been given murderers in the state of Pará, there was serious doubt that those involved with Dorothy's death would be convicted. People feared that the ranchers would get away with her murder. As the BBC reported,

> The state of Pará has a history marked by impunity in relation to crimes which occur in rural areas. The CPT (Bishops' Pastoral Land Commission) in Pará presented a report to the president of the State Tribunal for Justice which related that of the 774 murders which occurred in the state in the past 35 years, about 70% of cases did not have any sort of investigation over who was responsible for the crimes. No one involved with ordering crimes has been sentenced and served their punishment behind bars.

The U.S. State Department also requested of the Brazilian government that those responsible for Dorothy's death be brought to justice. It was reported that two United States FBI agents were sent to Brazil to help the local authorities pursue the murderers and those responsible. The international community was watching the proceedings carefully. Nevertheless, the judges in the state of Pará convinced the federal judges that they could handle the case and assured them that justice would be done.

On December 9, 2005, Raifran and Clodoaldo were brought to trial. They had changed their story from the time they were arrested. Originally, the two men had said that Raifran shot Dorothy in self-defense, thinking she was pulling out a gun instead of her Bible. That was the story the lawyers hired by Bida had told them to use for their defense. But Raifran realized that he was being made the scapegoat for the murder. Instead, he admitted that he and Clodoaldo had been paid to kill Dorothy and he named all the people involved. After describing what had happened, Raifran reenacted the murder for the police, who filmed the whole scene. The film was later shown on CNN. In fact, the two men refused the services of the lawyers hired by Bida and chose, instead, the public defender. Raifran named Tato as the representative of the ranchers who had paid for the crime. Both gunmen then named the ranchers, Vitalmiro Bastos de Moura, or "Bida," and Regivaldo Pereira Galvão as the ones who had ordered the murder. On December 10, the jury handed down a verdict of first degree murder for Raifran and a verdict of murder against Clodoaldo for conspiracy in the crime. Raifran was sentenced to twenty-seven years in prison and Clodoaldo to seventeen. The maximum punishment for murder in Brazil is thirty years.

A crowd of over two hundred protesters, farmers, and activists had camped outside the courthouse in Belém during the trial, demanding justice for Dorothy. The convictions of the two murderers were seen as the first step in bringing about justice in the state of Pará. People sang, prayed, and rejoiced when they heard the jury's decision. It was assumed that the other three men involved in paying for and planning Dorothy's killing would also face a jury trial. Senator Ana Julia Carepa, who headed the Senate Commission said, "This is the start. Now we're going to get the masterminds."

On April 26, 2006, Amair Feijoli da Cunha, also known as "Tato," who had been charged with being an intermediary in the murder of Sister Dorothy, was brought to court in Belém. When the two gunmen identified him as the one who had talked them into the crime and paid them, he, too, told the court the whole story of being charged with hiring the men to kill Dorothy. He too refused Bida's lawyers, was defended by a public defender, and proceeded to name the two ranchers who had provided the money. The jury found him guilty and he was sentenced to eighteen years in prison.

The two ranchers who had paid for the murder remained in jail awaiting trial. However, one of them, Regivaldo Galvão, had his lawyer go to Brasilia and plead for his release on the basis of habeas corpus. On June 29, 2006, the Supreme Federal Tribunal "acting contrary to all of the decisions of earlier courts who were closer to the case," granted habeas corpus to Regivaldo Pereira Galvão, meaning he would await his trail in liberty.

Galvão's release was considered a major setback in what had begun to be perceived as a case illustrating the possibility of achieving justice in the state of Pará. One of the judges involved in the trial of the gunmen affirmed that "liberty for this businessman, who led the consortium of people involved in the murder of Sister Dorothy, aside from being an affront, is a threat to workers, leaders, and human rights defenders in the region. This liberty certainly will be enjoyed by intimidating witnesses against the suspects." Furthermore, it was obvious that Galvão had sufficient funds to flee the region and the country, something that other wealthy men involved with murdering the poor farmers had done in the past. Consequently, the special secretary for human rights, Minister Paulo Vannuchi, petitioned the Court of Justice in Pará to speed up the trial of Galvão, and Bida, whose own petition for habeas corpus had been denied, keeping him in jail.

However, on May 14, 2007, Bida was brought to trial in Belém. The defense attorneys resorted to defaming Dorothy's character as their ploy to free their defendant. She was said to be an instrument of the United States, fomenting violence against the ranchers, providing guns to the farmers. The gunmen and Tato reversed the testimony previously offered in their trials naming Bida and Galvão as the instigators of the murder. They denied getting any money from the ranchers. This was not surprising, since everyone had expected the three men to have made deals with Bida before the trial. And yet the jury delivered a verdict of "guilty" for Bida. Judge Raimundo Moises Alves Flexa sentenced Bida to thirty years in jail, the maximum sentence for murder in Brazil. It was the first time in over seven hundred cases in Pará that a rancher who had ordered a killing was convicted. The farmers had some hope that justice could be obtained in Pará after all.

While the court was determining the fate of the murderers and dealing with those who were responsible for Dorothy's death, millions of people were hearing about the devotion and courage of the seventy-three-year-old sister who had given her life to the Amazon poor. Universities bestowed honorary doctorates on her, the United States Congress and the United Nations honored her, and programs of social justice were named for her. In each generation, there are those whose lives form and inform others who work for the poor. The story of Dorothy's life will continue to inspire countless numbers to take up her cause—not only in Brazil, but wherever there are people who experience the crush of oppression.

Dorothy was responsible for starting the Farmers' Union in her area, establishing over twenty-three schools where there were none, teaching sustainable farming techniques in her efforts to save the Amazon forest, and raising the consciousness of those who had yet to realize their rights. She demonstrated to all people what someone with faith, courage, and determination can do to change some part of the world desperately in need of justice.

Her story is far from over.

A PRAYER IN HONOR OF SISTER DOROTHY STANG

Adapted by Martin Sheen

Lord, make us instruments of your peace:

We are hidden away deep within ourselves trembling with fear in the face of such universal hatred, violence, and injustice.

Descend with us, Lord, into the depths of our powerlessness and fear and rekindle there the hope and power of your non-violent truth as we discover your fire for the second time. Then, Lord, call us forth and journey with us so that we may confront every wretched form of hatred, violence, and injustice with loving, nonviolent resistance.

Lord, make us instruments of your peace:

So that like our sister, Dorothy, we, too, may discover the path that unites the will of the spirit with the work of the flesh. Then may we, like her, fulfill the command of your prophet, Micah, to love greatly, do justice faithfully, and walk humbly with all our brothers and sisters.

Lord, make us instruments of your peace so that, like Dorothy, we may be made worthy of the long promised blessing received for the peacemaker. Then may we, like our sister, lift up a discarded third world and its entire people to a place

> "Where the heart is without fear
> and the head is held high, where knowledge is free,

Where the word has not been broken up into
fragments by narrow, domestic walls,

Where words come out from the depths of truth,

Where tireless striving stretches its arms to
perfection,

Where the clear stream of reason has not lost its
way into the dreary desert sands of dead habit,

Where the mind is led forward by thee into
ever-widening thought and action,

Into that heaven of freedom, my father,
let us all awake!"

Martin Sheen's remarks were inspired by the Prayer of St. Francis and Indian poet Rabindranath Tagore's work, sometimes referred to as "Mind without Fear."

A PARTIAL LIST OF HONORS
BESTOWED ON
SISTER DOROTHY STANG, S.N.D. de N.

Honorary Doctorates in Humane Letters:

Notre Dame de Namur University, Belmont, California	May, 2005
St. Joseph College, Renssalear, Indiana	May 2005
Santa Clara University, Santa Clara, California	June 2005
University of Dayton, Dayton, Ohio	February 2006

Commendations and Declarations:

Resolution 37 in the 109th Congress of the United States concurrent with the United States House of Representatives	May 23, 2005
Tribute to Sr. Dorothy Stang, United Nations	January 2006
Induction into the National Underground Railroad Freedom Center as an *Everyday Freedom Hero*, Cincinnati, Ohio	July 2006
Nominated for Tipperary Peace Committee Prize	December 2006

Honors in Brazil

Isa Cunha Medal for Services
Rendered to the Poor;
Legislative Assembly of the State of Pará   2004

Chico Mendes Award:
Honor for Heroes in the Struggle
for Life and Human Dignity;
Lawyers Organization of Brazil   December 2004

Woman of the Year Award for Human
Rights Municipal Council of Belém, Pará   August 3, 2005

Premio Aleceu Amoroso Lima
for Defense of Human Rights   2005

SOURCES

Nearly all the references used in this book are from primary sources, such as letters, interviews with those who knew Dorothy, and reports sent back to the Sisters of Notre Dame Province Center in Cincinnati, Ohio. I was also able to interview her brother and sisters, and to conduct further interviews with those who knew her in Arizona and the Amazon. Specific references appear below.

1. CALLED TO MISSION
Quotations from St. Julie Billiart, from Frances Rosner, SND and Lucy Tinsely, SND, *The Letters of St. Julie Billiart* (Rome: Gregorian Press, 1974), 141.

2. ARIZONA INTERLUDE
Description of Most Holy Trinity Parish, from a Jubilee publication by the parish, 1976.
Memories of Dorothy on the train to Arizona: Personal correspondence of Sr. Ruth Ellen Evers, SND (Sr. Ann Timothy), February 12, 2006.
Memories of Dorothy and *Mad* magazine, and story of a sick migrant baby, from personal correspondence of Nancy Clingan, undated.
Memories of Jim Mitchell, from private correspondence, May 31, 2006.

3. BRAZIL BEGINNINGS
Gustavo Gutiérrez, quoted in Judith Dwyer et al., eds., *The New Dictionary of Catholic Social Thought* (Collegeville, MN: Liturgical Press, 1994), 550.

Memories of Barbara English, SND, "Dorothy Stang, SND: Pioneer Woman," personal correspondence, 2006.

Memories of Sr. Joan Krimm, SND, from personal letter, Good Friday, 1967.

Dorothy's memories, "On weekends we used to go to interior," quoted by Sr. Barbara English, SND.

4. BLESSED ARE THE POOR

Dorothy, "So while the other SNDs were recuperating," quoted by Sr. Barbara English, SND, "Until the Song Is Sung," private printing, p. 55.

Dorothy, "The people felt they were missioning me," quoted by Sr. Barbara English, SND.

5. DEEPER INTO THE FOREST

Background on Brazilian development in the Amazon, see Miguel Carter, director, "Struggling for Sustainable Development in the Brazilian Amazon," research project for the class Micropolitics of Development, American University's School of International Service, Washington, DC, unpublished, 2006, p. 24.

Dorothy, "The people were very willing to work in community," and subsequent quotations, cited by Sr. Barbara English, SND.

Letter of Dorothy from Brazil, January 8, 1981, Province Publications of the Ohio Province, Reading, Ohio.

6. ON THE TRANSAMAZON

Dorothy describing work in early days in Pará: Interview with Sr. Barbara English, SND, 2003.

Memories of Brother Geronimo, from letter to Milton R. Medrau, shared with the author on June 9, 2006, in Altamira.

7. HUNGER FOR JUSTICE

"Their life expectancy is lower than it is in southern Brazil," interview with Sergio Trindade in Miguel Carter, director, "Struggling for Sustainable Development in the Brazilian

Amazon," research project for the class Micropolitics of Development, American University's School of International
Service, Washington, DC, unpublished, 2006, pp. 35–36.

Story of Joanna and her family, interview, Anapu, June 6, 2006.

Story of Maria and the Sisters of Notre Dame, interview, June
13, 2006.

Story of Sandra and Sisters of Notre Dame, interview, June 16,
2006.

8. LOVE OF CREATION

Information on the Earth Summit is available on the Internet.

Information on Matthew Fox and Creation Spirituality from
Rosemary R. Ruether, "Creation Spirituality: The Message
and the Movement," *Creation Spirituality*, November/
December 1990.

Memories of Dorothy at the program at Holy Names College from
Sharon Abercrombie, "Nun, Amazon Advocate, Murdered,"
The Catholic Voice, Vol. 43, No. 4, February 21, 2005, 1–2.

Dorothy, "When the priest came, he celebrated Mass..." This
and most of the quotations in this chapter come from a personal interview with Sr. Dorothy Stang by Sr. Barbara English during her visit to Brazil in 2003.

9. BLESSED ARE THE PERSECUTED

Memories of Michael Sepulveda, from personal correspondence,
July 23, 2006.

Dorothy's "letter" to St. Julie Billiart and Françoise Blin de
Bourbon, written from Anapu, September 3, 1998, and discovered in August 2006.

10. UNLESS A SEED DIE

Memories of Samuel Clements, from the website for his project,
"The Student, the Nun & the Amazon":
www.studentnunamazon.com.

Bishop Erwin Krautler's memory of Luis: From a homily by
Bishop Krautler, bishop of Xingu, at a memorial service at
the site of Dorothy's murder.

Memory of Francisca, "I am here today for Dorothy," interview on June 7, 2006.

Dorothy's call to her brother, from David Stang, "Martyred in the Rain Forest," *Maryknoll* magazine, July/August 2005.

Quotations from Ivan and Gabriel, from interview, June 8, 2006.

11. A SEED PLANTED

The dialogue between Dorothy and her murderers is taken from "The Request for Transfer of Jurisdiction," by the Office of Legal Affairs of the State of Pará, submitted by Claudo Fonteles, Brasilia, March 3, 2005.

Threatening message to Gabriel, cited in "Response of the Government of Brazil," June 25, 2005.

The account of the events following the murder were recorded for the Sisters of Notre Dame by Sr. Jo Ann Depweg, Sr. Rita Raboin, and Sr. Ani Wihby and entitled "Sacred Moments, Special People."

Greenpeace: The environmental organization has produced two programs telling the story of Dorothy's murder. "Dorothy Vive" is a 2006 title.

EPILOGUE

BBC News, June 29, 2006, "Suspect in Dorothy Stang Murder Trial Set Free."

Senator Julia Carepa, quoted on BBC News, "The Day After," December 11, 2005.